DELETE TH@T

DELETE TH@T

REMOVE Negative Patterns from Your Mind, Mouth & Movement. *ROOT-OUT* The Past, **REWRITE** The Present *and REWIRE* Your Future.

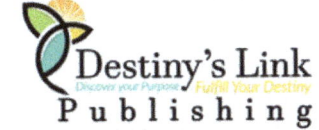

Destiny's Link Publishing
Orlando, Florida

DELETE TH@T

© 2025 Sandra 'DEE' Daley

All rights reserved. No part of this publication may be reproduced, stored in a retrieval system, or transmitted in any form or by any means, electronic, mechanical, photocopying, recording, or otherwise, without the prior written permission of the publisher.

Published in Orlando, Florida, by Destiny's Link Publishing, an imprint of Destiny's Link Publishing, Destiny's Link Publishing, titles may be purchased in bulk for educational, business, fund-raising, or sales promotional use. For information, please e-mail info@deenterprise.com.

Scripture quotations marked KJV are taken from the King James Version. Public domain.

Any Internet addresses, phone numbers, or company or product information printed in this book are offered as a resource and are not intended in any way to be or to imply an endorsement by Destiny's Link Publishing, nor does Destiny's Link Publishing vouch for the existence, content, or services of these sites, phone numbers, companies, or products beyond the life of this book.

ISBN: 978-0-9898425-3-2

Design and layout by Sandra 'DEE' Daley

DELETE TH@T

DELETE TH@T

About The Author

Sandra Daley is a lover of God and God's people. Jesus is the head of her life. and she lives every day to please him. Anyone that knows her well will testify that she loves the Lord more than anything. Sandra puts God first, her marriage second, her children and family next, then ministry, then her work, passions and purpose.

Born and raised in Antigua, Caribbean, Daley migrated to the United States in her teen years. Sandra Daley is an Entrepreneur, Author and Philanthropist. Sandra is married for 38 years with two children and six grandchildren. She earned her Bachelor of Science Degree in Computer Science from the University of California, Irvine, and a Master of Science Degree in Project Management from St. Edwards University, Austin, Texas.

Sandra professional experience includes software and systems engineering, quality assurance, and program management. Daley held various management positions at prominent companies such as Boeing and Raytheon Technologies. Her peers, employees, customers, and competitors alike, have praised her as a relentless and intentional overachiever.

As an Entrepreneur, Sandra is the Founder and CEO of

DELETE TH@T

Destiny Executive Enterprise, LLC (DEE, Inc - www.deenterprise.com.). DEE, Inc., is a multi-faceted company that is responsible for publishing books selling on Amazon (e.g. 24/7 God: Practical Prayer Guide, DESTINY COLLABORATORS: Discover The Secrets To Successful Collaborative & Committed Connections), & now **DELETE TH@T book**. Sandra is known for her motivational and inspirational products (e.g. 365 Daily Calendar), Multiple Mobile Apps (e.g. Personality Assessment, Name Meaning, Business Coaching, etc.). Currently, Sandra is working on releasing a series of books on ALTARS: The Matter of The Heart (Addressing Born-Again Christians heart condition towards God).

Sandra currently and her husband serve their community as pastors for the DESTINY House of Prayer for Everyone (D-Hope) (www.d-hope.org). Feel free to contact Sandra at 951-283-1681or sandra@deenterprise.com for any questions and speaking opportunities.

Acknowledgment

I want to thank the following people who have encouraged me and helped me complete this project:

Jesus, the author and finisher of my faith, for giving me the inspiration to begin, loving nudges to continue, and strength to finish.

Spouse (H. Daley, Sr.), my best friend, the love of my life, and the great father of my children. Thanks for providing me with unwavering support and for loving me when I was unlovable.

Creative - Ai Assisted: This book is Spirit-led, human-authored, and AI-assisted.

This book is the inspiration of me, the author: Sandra 'DEE' Daley. Every idea, message, teaching, chapter layout, and visual concept found within these pages was conceived by and spiritually inspiration of the Holy Spirit to me.

To bring the vision to life with excellence and precision, I utilized the power of AI as a creative assistant, as a tool to help shape and express the content I thought of. Through intentional prompts, spiritual insight, and clear direction, the author guided AI to assist in editing, refining, and formatting the book's content, as an extension of my voice, not a replacement.

From concept to content to cover, this book reflects my original revelation into thoughts that came from God through HIS Spirit.

PREFACE

It all began with a simple text message. I was mid-conversation, thumbing out my usual response, when I typed the words: "I don't have any..." And then it happened. Clear as day, I heard the Spirit say: "DELETE THAT."

It wasn't just a whisper, but it reverberated deep in my soul. You know when something hits you so hard it bypasses your brain and settles right in your *"Shanananana"*? (That's my way of saying "both in my spirit man & soul,") It is that moment when the spiritual realm sparked something in me. It wasn't the first time, and I knew it wasn't just a correction; it was an invitation.

I paused, deleted the message, and rewrote it from a different mental space and spiritual place. Same intention, but this time, from a position of power, not from a soul deficit. A message of truth, not defeat. Then the revelation flowed like water. I was beginning to understand the following:

"What a man thinks, so is he.

He speaks words that become decrees.

What he writes becomes policy.

And that's what other people see."

DELETE TH@T

That line kept echoing. And I started to see it all differently. You see, nothing just happens. Every thought, every word, every text, every post, it all starts with a root. Roots grow stems. Stems forms branches. Branches produce leaves. And eventually, those leaves bear fruit.

Writing is the fruit of that root. So when we write things like "I can't" or "I don't have," we are not simply venting we are issuing spiritual demands that the enemy is more than willing to fulfill.

We live in a world where we're constantly writing emails, social media posts, journal entries, text messages. But how often do we pause to think: What am I really declaring into existence? Our minds are like governments. Our spirits are cities. And our words? They are the policies that govern them both. Even the Bible says in Proverbs 25:28:

> "He that hath no rule over his own spirit is like a city that is broken down, and without walls."

When we erase a sentence, we're not just editing a message, we're canceling an assignment. When we delete a thought before it becomes a word, we're uprooting a root before it can bear bad fruit. And when we reframe our writing, we are literally rewriting our lives.

DELETE TH@T

That's what this book is about.
It's not just about words.
It's the world your words are creating.
It's not just about deleting text.
It's about deleting patterns.
It's not just about reframing thoughts.
It's about rewriting destiny.

This is a book, yes. But more than that it's your reset button. Though this book started with a text message and a whisper from God to rewrite the text, in that moment, I realized how often we unknowingly write and speak from a place of lack, limitation, comparison, competition and broken patterns inviting negativity to take root in our lives.

That divine interruption birthed the revelation behind this book for me to jot down my thoughts and help others like you to understand writing should not be a thoughtless action. What we write reveals what we think, and what we think governs what we become.

DELETE TH@T is your manual for spiritual editing, removing negative patterns from your mind, mouth, and movement, uprooting the past, rewriting the present, and rewiring your future. Each chapter gives you tools, truth, and activations to help you live free from toxic cycles and write a new policy for your

DELETE TH@T

life. My heart in writing this is simple, to help you recognize the power you carry, not just in what you say but in what you think and write. So, here's my invitation, take this journey with yourself and eradicate these negative patterns.

Read every word with intention.

And when anything rises that doesn't align with the future you're called to live, **DELETE TH@T** before it births something you cannot control.

DELETE TH@T

Table of Contents

About The Author iii
Acknowledgment v
PREFACE vi
Introduction 1
Control-Alt-Delete Your Life 1
Chapter 1 – REMOVE NEGATIVE PATTERNS 12

   1.1 Sister Mad-All-The-Time 17

   1.2 INVISIBLE: TOXIC THOUGHT LOOPS 19

      1.2.1 Childhood Toxic Mind Loop 21

      Science Confirms: Toxic Loops in the Womb 24

      Prayer: To Heal The WOMB 27

      Tracing Pre-Memory Emotional Patterns 28

      1.2.2 Influences Beyond the Home 28

      DECLARATION: Break Cultural and Family Cycles 33

      Prayer: Renounce Old Patterns 34

      1.2.3 PATHOLOGY: Genetics Inheritance 35

      EPIGENETICS: How Genes Work 36

      Breaking Negative Inherited 'Epigenetics' 39

      Identifying 'Real Life' Epigenetic Influence 40

      Healing Epigenetic Trauma 41

      Healing that reaches both realms 42

DELETE TH@T

    Passing Down Good Epigenetics............................ 45

    Surrendering Inherited Patterns for Healing........ 48

    Declaration: Healing Generational Trauma.......... 48

    TRAINING YOUR INNER VOICE.............................. 51

1.3 SELF-SABOTAGING SPEECH (MOUTH).......... 53

    Mouth: Microphone to the Spirit Realm 54

    Declaration: "I Take Back My Voice" 56

1.4 BEHAVIORAL CYCLES (MOVEMENT) 57

    Your Habits Are Thoughts Wearing Shoes............ 59

    Behavioral Cycles & Movement 64

    Prayer: **Thoughts** → **Words** → **Movement** 64

1.5 GOVERNMING ANOLOGY OF THE SOUL 67

    SOUL GOVERNMENT STATMENTS........................ 68

    SOUL GOVERNMENT PICTORAL DIAGRAM 68

    REFRAMING: Removing Negative Patterns 72

    Who's Ruling in My Soul? 73

1.6 SOUND SPIRITUAL FOUNDATION 74

    3-Gate Reflection: (Think–Speak–Write).............. 78

    DECLARATION: THINK - Gate Reflection............... 78

DELETE TH@T

DECLARATION: SPEAK - Gate Reflection 79

DECLARATION: WRITE - Gate Reflection 79

Chapter 2 – ROOT OUT THE PAST 82

   2.1 Trace the Source 84

      REAL-LIFE EXAMPLES & RELATED RESEARCH 89

      Example 1: Abandonment 89

      Example 2: Trauma 90

      Example 3: Rejection 92

      Example 4: Disappointment 94

      Residue: Generational & Emotional Cycles 96

      The Danger of Buried Pain 97

   2.2 Uncovering Emotional Roots 97

      Power Does Not Negotiate 98

      Don't Negotiate with Terrorists 99

      Don't Respond When You Get Upset 99

      God Requires That We Inquire 100

      Offense Is Rooted in Our Self Image 101

      OFFENSE: Invitation to REFLECT and REFINE 103

      The Closer to God, the fewer the Words 104

      Tracing The Roots 105

DELETE TH@T

Prayer: Search My Roots 107

2.3 Detoxing: Soul from Memory Triggers 107

Spiritual Excavation – PRAYER GUIDE 110

Spiritual Excavation Mindset 111

2.3.1 Healing Soul Wounds................................ 112

Forgetfulness vs. Inability to Recall 116

Prayer to Reclaim Your Soul 119

Prayer: Memory Triggers Detachment 124

Chapter 3 – REWRITE THE PRESENT 127

3.1 Power of Present-Tense Authority 127

Rewriting Self-Talk and Identity Statements 127

Example 1: Rewriting Dating Self-Talk 129

Example 2: Miscarriages 130

Example 3: Divorce 131

Example 4: Parenting 132

3.2 Rewriting Policies in Your Inner Man 135

3.1.1 Your Mind Drafts the Law 136

3.1.2 Capture What Is Trying to Capture You .. 138

Legislative Thought Tracker 140

DELETE TH@T

    3.1.3   Your Mouth Decrees the Law 140

    3.1.4   Your Movement Enforces the Law 141

    I DECLARE: Reclaim Authority 143

    Prayer: Enforce Authority 145

    Intentional Self-Healing Language 145

    Discernment Detector 146

Chapter 4: REWIRE YOUR FUTURE 149

    Write A Future Self Script 152

    4.1.   The Science of Neuroplasticity 154

    Vignette 1: Sister Twisted-Mind Brain Rewiring. 155

    Vignette 2: Forming Spiritual Highways 158

    Vignette 3: Old Memories-Blocking New Love ... 163

    Vignette 4: Repetition=Spiritual Acceleration 164

    4.2.   Spiritual Acceleration 165

    4.3.   Spiritual Renewal 168

    4.3.1.   The Domino Effect of Deletion 173

    Rewire Your Thoughts 175

    4.3.2.   ROOT: Once Produced is Disrupted 175

    4.4.   Designing Your Environment 177

DELETE TH@T

    4.4.1.   THE RESET 180

    4.4.2.   RESET PRAYER CARDS 182

        PRAYER CARD 1: Deleting Negative Patterns 182

        PRAYER CARD 2: ROOT IT OUT 183

        PRAYER CARD 3: WRITE IT RIGHT 183

        PRAYER CARD 5: RESET THE STANDARD 185

        PRAYER CARD 6: SILENCE THE SABOTEUR 185

        PRAYER CARD 7: CLEAN THE ALTAR 186

CONCLUSION: Delete It for Good 188
ACTIVITIES & EXERCISES 190

    ACTIVITY 1: Tracing Pre-Memory Patterns 190

    EXERCISE 2: Passing Good Epigenetics 191

    EXERCISE 3: Healing Inherited Patterns 192

    ACTIVITY 4: DELETE TH@T – Language 193

    EXERCISE 5: 7-DAY Anti-Self-Sabotage 194

    ACTIVITY 6: Behavioral Cycles & Movement 196

    EXERCISE 7: Behavior vs. Belief Alignment 197

    ACTIVITY 8: Who's Ruling in My Soul? 198

    ACTIVITY 9: 3-Gate Reflection 199

    ACTIVITY 10: Spiritual Excavation 201

DELETE TH@T

ACTIVITY 11: Trace The Root 203

ACTIVITY 12: Legislation Thought Tracker............. 205

ACTIVITY 13: Self-Healing Language 205

ACTIVITY 14: DISCERNMENT DETECTOR 206

ACTIVITY 15: Future Self Script 208

ACTIVITY 16: VISUAL PRAYER CARDS 1-7 209

Bibliography 211

Introduction

Control-Alt-Delete Your Life

It started like any other day emails, texts, scrolling, replying. I was in mid-conversation, thumbing out a message on my phone. Without thinking, I typed the words, "I don't have any…" And at that moment, everything changed. I heard a voice so clear, so piercing, it bypassed my mind and hit my spirit: "DELETE THAT." It wasn't a suggestion. It was a command from Heaven.

I paused. Stared at my phone. And something in me knew this wasn't about grammar or word choice. it was about alignment. I had just unintentionally agreed with something from the enemy's camp, but I didn't quite know what it was yet. I had written a line that partnered with limitation. And the Spirit of God interrupted my habit to rewrite my outcome. Right there, I erased the words and reframed my message. Not out of fear but out of revelation. That simple moment sparked what you're now holding in your hands or what you are reading on your digital device. A

INTRODUCTION

bold journey to delete what doesn't align, uproot what no longer serves, and rewrite your life from the inside out. Thus, the reason for 'Control-Alt-Delete' for our lives. The change must be made from the inside out.

The Control-Alt-Delete (often written as Ctrl + Alt + Del) command is a well-known keyboard shortcut function in Windows operating systems. Many of us with a Personal Computer (PC) is familiar with this function. When we press Control-Alt-Delete the Security Options Screen (Windows) immediately displays and brings up the Lock your computer; Switch users; Log out; Open the Task Manager; Change your password; reboot the system or force a hard reset; Force Interrupt / Emergency Reset (Legacy use) it was used to force a system reboot if the computer was frozen. (e.g. On some systems, pressing it twice would trigger a hard reset); and Task Manager Shortcut, often used to access Task Manager when an application is unresponsive, or the system is slow. This allows you to end processes that are malfunctioning.

In a metaphorical or spiritual sense, Control-Alt-Delete represents a divine interruption, a reset of our mind, mouth, or movement. '**CONTROL [<CTRL>]** can be seen as us taking back control of our thoughts. The '**<Alt>**' (Alternate) is how we choose alternate beliefs, words, or action. And '**<delete>**' is how we remove what no longer serves or aligns with our divine purpose. Exercised individually or together, they are powerful symbolic parallel for reclaiming authority over our internal operating system.

Each Control-Alt-Delete system function also has a parallel life connection to our internal/spiritual system through the lens of *DELETE TH@T*. For example, let's review each **Control-Alt-Delete Functions.**

The '**Lock**' Your Computer function on the keyboard, prevents others from accessing the system without permission; requires a password to unlock. In life Sometimes, you need to *lock down your mind, heart, or emotions* from outside influences, distractions, or toxic patterns. Spiritually, it means setting boundaries, safeguarding your thoughts, and securing your identity in Christ. You're not giving access to just anyone or any thought.

INTRODUCTION

The '**Switch Users**' function allows a different user to log into the system without shutting it down or losing progress. In life, there are moments when you need to shift your internal identity switching from the "wounded self" to the "healed self," or from "victim mode" to "victory mode." It's about stepping into the version of yourself that aligns with purpose and destiny without erasing your growth.

The '**Log Out**' function ends the current session and closes all personal data and programs. In life, there are soul ties, cycles, or emotional states you need to log out of. Logging out spiritually means releasing what's no longer serving you be it toxic relationships, false beliefs, or outdated assignments. You can't start a new chapter if you're still signed into the old one.

The open the '**Task Manager**' function allow users to view all running programs and processes, see which ones are using resources, and end unresponsive tasks. It is a fast way to improve performance. When you feel overwhelmed or sluggish in your faith, emotions, or purpose, *DELETE TH@T* acts like a spiritual shortcut to clarity. It helps you identify what's draining your peace or potential and empowers you to take back control quickly. In life, this is your self-audit moment. Spiritually, you're opening the "task manager" of your soul to ask allowing the Holy Spirit to list all current and active actions and thoughts. You will be able to see and monitor: What thoughts are running in the background? What's draining my energy? What needs to be shut down? It's a tool for identifying and ending toxic thought patterns.

The '**Change Your Password**' function allow users to update the security key used to access the system. In life, when we change our password, this symbolizes a shift in access and authority. What is used to get into your heart or mind no longer has clearance. This means the access to your buttons and triggers are changed or moved so that the enemy no longer have access to push our buttons. Spiritually, this means updating your declarations, renewing your beliefs, and changing the "code" to who and what you allow to speak into your life.

The '**Force Interrupt / Emergency Reset**' function is used when the system is frozen or non-

INTRODUCTION

responsive and allows users to force a shutdown and reboot. Sometimes, our life hits a point where nothing's moving. We feel like we are emotionally stuck, spiritually frozen. That's when God steps in with a divine emergency reset. It may feel abrupt, but it's necessary to restore function and clarity. This is the moment where *DELETE TH@T* becomes a lifeline. We now follow the direction of the Holy Spirit. We may start to write something but quickly erase it. <CTRL-ALT-DELET> is our internal System Reset and it matters how we use and access it.

Just like your computer needs regular management to keep running smoothly, your inner life, your thoughts, your emotions, your behaviors also needs intentional resets. *DELETE TH@T* is that spiritual Control-Alt-Delete. It gives you the awareness, authority, and activation to clear out what's unresponsive, misaligned, or dangerous to your destiny. You're not just maintaining your system, you're mastering it.

Just like a frozen computer system requires a reset, sometimes your inner world your thoughts, words, and actions need a divine interruption. That's where the spiritual meaning of *Control-Alt-Delete* comes in. You're not just here to clean up the mess you're here to reset the system entirely. This is a bold journey to delete what doesn't align, uproot what no longer serves, and rewrite your life from the inside out. Much like a keyboard command used to regain control over a locked or broken computer, God is inviting you to hit your own spiritual *Control-Alt-Delete*.

DELETE TH@T is a 'Divine' system reset for your mind, your mouth, and your movement. The moment where heaven steps in and halts your hand mid-sentence. It's the divine interruption you didn't know you needed to confront negative patterns, unearth toxic roots, and code your future with Heaven's strategy. Not just to protect your future, but to expose your inner programming. When you delete something in the natural, like a text, a social media post, or a journal entry, it may feel like a small act. But if you pause long enough to ask ***why***, why you wrote those words, why you were about to send that message, why your spirit suddenly tightened you'll realize that your

INTRODUCTION

writing isn't random. It's fruit from a root. Words are not just letters on a page; they are policies drafted by the internal government of your soul. They are decrees authorized by thoughts, which are often silently governed by the deeper, unseen laws etched in your heart.

When God stops you from completing that thought, that sentence, that email, it's not just to censor you it's to show you something about yourself. Something you may not even know is living beneath the surface. A belief. A fear. A hurt. A memory. A mindset. If you have the discipline to sit in that divine interruption and ask, "What root made me write this?" **You won't just delete words; you'll begin uprooting the source.**

That's where transformation happens. Not just at the surface of deleted text, but in the soul surgery that follows your obedience. DELETE TH@T isn't about erasing for the sake of silence it's about deleting to make space for divine clarity, correction, and ultimately, completion in God's will. And that my friends started me on this journey and what will help you to start and complete your own DELETE TH@T journey.

Here's what you're about to learn and encounter:

Chapter 1: Remove Negative Patterns from Your Mind, Mouth & Movement

You'll learn how your internal world writes the script for your external life. This chapter introduces an activity to help you assess your thought patterns, speech habits, and behavior cycles. You'll discover how casual words like "I can't" and "I don't have" are spiritual decrees and how to replace them with truth that aligns with who God says you are.

Chapter 2: Root Out the Past

We go beneath the surface. You'll trace your pain, patterns, and beliefs back to their roots, trauma, childhood wounds, generational cycles, and spiritual agreements you didn't know you made. You'll be guided through a process of excavation using tools like journaling, prayer altars, and guided reflection to pull out what's been hidden and give it over to God.

Chapter 3: Rewrite the Present

INTRODUCTION

Now that you've cleared the weeds, you'll learn to create a different way of thinking, speaking and writing through the language and leading of the Holy Spirit. This chapter empowers you to create declarations, affirmations, and daily rituals that align with your healed identity. You'll take your place as the lawmaker of your inner government. Writing policies of purpose, peace, and progress. You'll learn to stop copying and pasting old scripts of your tattered soul and start creating new narratives that flow from the mind of God for your life.

Chapter 4: Rewire Your Future

Finally, you'll reprogram your destiny by rewiring your mind. Using spiritual imagination, vision scripting, habit creation, and prophetic decrees, you'll step into the role of author over your future. You'll learn how to build an environment that supports your transformation and walk in the power of faith + works. You'll delete the old code and write new software for your soul.

This is your Control-Alt-Delete moment.

You're not here by accident.

You were divinely interrupted to reimagine what's possible. So, take a deep breath. Get your pen ready. And the next time a lie tries to write your story, you'll know exactly what to do. You will...

DELETE TH@T

Chapter 1 – REMOVE NEGATIVE PATTERNS

Have you ever gone through a breakup with someone you genuinely believed was "the one"? Do you even remember? When did this happen? What did you do?

For many, breakups don't just represent the end of a relationship they represent the collapse of a mental and emotional future that had already been imagined, visualized, and, in many ways, emotionally "lived in." For women, research shows that they often form deep emotional connections earlier in relationships, and their brains begin to associate the partnership with long-term security and fulfillment **(Morris & Reiber, 2011)**. Basically, the emotional reactions to breakups among men and women are different. Women tend to experience more acute emotional pain initially, while men tend to experience more delayed emotional grief.

Morris and Rieber updated and expanded their research in their 2017 published study where they found that women are more likely to report higher emotional distress following a breakup, not just because of the relationship itself, but because of the emotional investments and **mental rehearsals of the future** wedding plans, family scenarios, and shared life moments. Neurologically, the female brain releases **oxytocin** the referred to as the "bonding hormone" during intimate and emotionally significant moments, which cements the sense of connection and future planning even more deeply. So, when a relationship ends, it isn't just the loss of a person it's the **internal collapse of a vision**, a psychological trauma akin to grief.

For men, the impact is often quieter but equally profound. Studies, including one from *The Journal of Men's Health*, indicate that while men may not express emotional devastation as readily, they often experience delayed psychological effects because they had attached identity and future aspirations to their partner (Oliffe, et al. 2019). In many cases, a man may have already mentally "seen himself" growing old with his chosen partner. The breakup, therefore, sever not just a bond but a constructed sense of self and stability. The male brain, while less likely to immediately release oxytocin, still experiences a decline in dopamine and serotonin, key neurotransmitters tied to motivation, joy, and focus leading to depressive symptoms and an overall emotional crash.

It seems like the combination of hormonal, neurological, and psychological interplay often causes both men and women to develop negative patterns post-breakup. These breakups generate distrust, self-sabotage, emotional detachment, harsh self-criticism, or even "vows" like *"I'll never trust anyone again."* These patterns, once repeated, become ingrained not just emotionally, but neurologically. And cause people to act irrationally. In some cases, both men and women write a lot of things out of that pain and feeling of loss.

Have you written out of your pain?

Have you written something that you had to delete?

Have you written something and which you could go back and DELETE TH@T?

According to the principles of neuroplasticity (Kays, Hurley, & Taber 2012), the brain strengthens the connections it uses most. That means negative thought cycles can become hardwired into the brain over time, forming unconscious belief systems that guide future relationships and self-perception. The key to erasing these negative patterns lies in interrupting the cycle through conscious awareness, spiritual healing, and intentional reprogramming. This process reduces and in time eliminates the number of 'deletes' for it delete the source of the emotional pain that produces the negative pattern.

But first, individuals must identify the belief or emotional repeats that look like a software 'loop' code that have them fallen into what they have been telling themselves since the breakup? It will help to break up what they begin to believe about love, relationships, or their own worth? Once this is done the person will be able to move on and engage in pattern disruption.

Pattern disruption using spiritual practices (such as prayer, declarations, or inner healing sessions), therapeutic journaling, and behavioral interventions like cognitive reframing. With reframing, a person learns how to reframe their point of view, belief systems and emotional triggers. After this, they will be able to replace the old narrative with new truth that ultimately helps them to choose a suitable and compatible mate. Drawing from the research of Fisher, Aron, and Brown (2006), romantic love activates the same mammalian brain systems associated with reward, motivation, and addiction. Specifically, those rich in **dopamine**, the neurotransmitter that fuels desire and pursuit.

When someone falls in love, the brain begins to hardwire emotional significance to that person, forming strong mental associations that impact memory, behavior, and future decision-making. This neurochemical wiring explains why, when relationships go wrong or end abruptly, individuals often write things they later regret. Also, emotional outbursts, irrational declarations, or desperate pleas that reflect the brain's distress response rather than divine wisdom. These written expressions are symptoms of deeper neurological and emotional patterns formed during the love-bonding process. However, through various pattern disruption techniques (prayer, declarations, and inner healing), therapeutic journaling, and cognitive reframing individuals can begin to reset these reward circuits. Cognitive reframing helps shift perspective, allowing the person to re-evaluate belief systems and emotional triggers that led them into unhealthy attachments in the first place. By replacing the old narrative with God's truth, the individual not only prevents the need to DELETE TH@T after-the-fact but becomes spiritually and emotionally equipped to choose a more suitable and compatible mate in accordance with the leading of the Holy Spirit. Relationships that align not with past pain, but with renewed purpose.

They can now speak and write the kind of love and life they believe they deserve, or what God ordained. This removal of negative patterns reinforces spiritual renewal and consistency and strengthen positive, repeated 'LOOP' actions. Healing is possible when we understand that the brain and the spirit can be renewed. As Romans 12:2 (KJV) reminds us, transformation comes 'by the **renewing of your mind**.' Science now confirms what the bible been proclaiming:

WHAT WE MEDITATE ON, WE MANIFEST.

1.1 Sister Mad-All-The-Time

When we erase the false narratives and rewrite with intention, we no longer live in the ruins of a broken vision. We walk in the clarity of a healed one.

To emphasis this the more let's examine a story that all of us can in some ways identify and relate to. Let's take a trip through the eyes of a fictitious character, I am calling **sister Mad-All-The-Time.**

Sister Mad-All-The-Time is a gifted writer who often finds herself journaling her pain. She just broke up with someone and had nowhere to place her frustrations, anguish and hatred. This is her fifth (5th) heartbreak in six years. After every breakup she uses her journaling gift to write down the experience but in an unhealthy way. After every breakup or disappointment, she would pen bitter, angry thoughts like, *"I'm not lovable,"* or *"Everyone leaves me."* However, this last breakup is so painful that her heart ache is so bad that it cannot be contained in just a book. So, she took it to social media and journaled her thoughts and rants for all to see. Not once did she consider the consequences. Her pain blinded any rational or godly thoughts. DELETE TH@T had no chance because her pain flowed from a space far out of reach from the strokes of her fingers. Sister Mad-All-The-Time didn't realize that her writing wasn't just cathartic, it was reinforcing a spiritual narrative.

Her words were not innocent, they were agreements.

One night, after typing out yet another page of heartbreak, she felt a holy pause. Something nudged her to **DELETE TH@T**. She stared at the screen, confused. "It's just journaling," she thought. But the Spirit whispered,

"Those words are becoming your prophecy."

In obedience, she erased the entire entry and instead wrote a declaration: *"I am loved by God, chosen for purpose, and healing in truth."* That was the beginning of her freedom. The more Sister Mad-All-The-Time caught and corrected the negative narratives, the more her heart healed. The more Sister Mad-All-The-Time work on herself she transforms into Sister Managed-Emotions. This is story reveals spiritual science in action. When you remove the pattern, you remove its power to manifest, and you align yourself with the destiny heaven already wrote about you.

The spiritual science behind removing negative patterns, and it's rooted in the divine law of sowing and reaping, thought and manifestation, spirit and consequence. In the realm of the spirit, nothing is neutral. Every thought is a seed, every word is a blueprint, and every action is a command. Negative patterns are not just bad habits; they are spiritual systems that have taken root in the soul through repetition, trauma, or inherited beliefs.

These patterns attract familiar spirits and demonic activity because the enemy thrives on cycles that keep us bound. The act of removing a negative pattern is not simply about willpower, it's about divine partnership. It requires **identifying the entry point**, repenting for agreement, renouncing the lie, and replacing it with God's truth. Spiritually, this reprograms your inner operating system and evicts anything that's been feeding off your dysfunction. The moment you interrupt that cycle even once you send a signal to heaven that you're ready to live free, and a signal to hell that the old contract is canceled.

1.2 INVISIBLE: TOXIC THOUGHT LOOPS

Have you ever stopped mid-sentence and asked yourself, "Why did I just say that?" Or caught yourself thinking the same toxic thought on repeat like a broken record? The truth is, we live from the inside out. Your thoughts create your world. Your words reinforce it. Your actions manifest it. We go from **Thoughts → Words → Actions.** It may seem like it is all in the mind but many of us are trapped in invisible cages of toxic thought loops cycles of fear, insecurity, scarcity, and shame that subtly (and not so subtly) dictate our beliefs. Thoughts like, *"I'm not enough," "It never works out for me,"* or *"People always leave,"* become the blueprint for how we interpret life. And before we know it, we're not just thinking about them, we're speaking to them and then writing them. That is why developing a DELETE TH@T mindset is necessary. And until you become aware of what's been playing in the background of your mind, you'll keep living out scripts you didn't consciously choose.

The Bible says in *Psalm 139:2*, "You understand my thoughts from afar," revealing a powerful truth that God doesn't just hear what we think, HE sees the source of our thinking. This means that thoughts are not the genesis of our mental activity. They don't appear from nowhere. Instead, thoughts are the fruit of deeper **roots** invisible mind loops influenced by various sources that often go unexamined. From early childhood, we are shaped by what we were taught, what we observed, and what was modeled for us whether healthy or dysfunctional. Our culture, upbringing, family systems, and repeated words spoken around us (or to us) become **the programming code** that informs us of our mental framework. Pathology also plays a role: unhealed traumas, genetic predispositions, or patterns of anxiety or fear passed down through generations can color how we interpret reality.

These geneses of our thoughts play a role in shaping the mental and spiritual loop that ultimately becomes our lived behavior. For example:

1.2.1 Childhood Toxic Mind Loop

formed by What We Were Taught, Observed, and Modeled. From the moment we are born, our brains act like **sponges**, absorbing everything we see, hear, and feel. The way our caregivers respond to stress, speak to others, treat us, or even handle failure. As a matter of fact, there is a deeper fascinating and foundational concept when understanding the early origins of thought formation. You see Long before a baby takes its first breath, learning has already begun. In the third trimester, around 25 to 28 weeks gestation, the baby's auditory system becomes functional, and by 32 weeks, the fetus can hear and respond to sounds with more consistency.

What does this mean? A baby in the womb can hear the mother's voice, the rhythm of her speech, the tone of her emotions, and even patterns of music or language spoken frequently. Studies on *Learning-induced neural plasticity of speech processing before birth by* researchers Partanen, Kujala, Näätänen, et al. published in: *Proceedings of the National Academy of Sciences of the United States of America (PNAS),* 2013 have shown that newborns recognize melodies, voices, and speech patterns they were exposed to in utero. Demonstrating that memory, recognition, and even basic auditory learning begins in the womb. But it's more than just sound. Babies are also influenced by the emotional climate of the womb.

Research by Vivette Glover (2014), explores how **maternal stress** and elevated cortisol levels during pregnancy can impact fetal development, particularly the baby's future emotional and cognitive health. Dr. Glover's research demonstrates that how anxiety during pregnancy can cross the placental barrier and affect fetal brain development, especially in areas related to emotional regulation and stress response.

Glover's findings are foundational in the field of prenatal programming, providing scientific evidence that the emotional state of the mother can have long-term impacts on the mental health and behavioral patterns of the child. Her research shows how fetal programming and prenatal psychology suggests that high levels of maternal stress, trauma, or anxiety can release cortisol and other stress hormones into the womb environment. These chemical signals inform the baby's developing nervous system about what kind of world they are about to enter. If a fetus experiences prolonged exposure to fear, conflict, or rejection even unintentionally, it can prime the brain to be more reactive to stress after birth.

In essence, the womb becomes the classroom of

emotional and neurological programming. That is why it is so important that adults, not just the mother carrying the child in her womb, must create a safe environment for all. For if the adult in the environment is already corrupt and captured then the environment is going to reflect the dominant thought patterns. Since the genesis of the thought patterns are often invisible the adults themselves are not even aware of the toxicity they are cultivating. Then the child in the womb will not only be born into sin, already having the sin nature from the womb but also from the womb is being shaped into iniquity. Did you ever think it possible that a baby in the womb could be affected in such a way? Even the bible gave us a hint that this was possible.

In John 9:1–3 *(NIV)*, the disciples ask Jesus a striking question as they pass a man born blind. *"Rabbi, who sinned, this man or his parents, that he was born blind?" Jesus answered, 'Neither this man nor his parents sinned, but this happened so that the works of God might be displayed in him.'"* This moment reveals a few critical truths. First, it reflects an ancient Jewish belief that sin could influence a fetus in utero, or that children could be punished for the sins of their parents. Interestingly, Jesus does not dismiss the idea that prenatal influence is real, but rather clarifies that ***in this specific case***, the blindness wasn't caused by personal or ancestral sin it was permitted for a divine demonstration of healing. That distinction is powerful. While not all conditions are caused by sin or trauma, Scripture and science agree that the womb is a spiritually and biologically formative environment. In fact, the disciples' question indirectly confirms what modern science has now validated. That is, a child can be shaped by the spiritual and emotional state of their parents, even before birth.

Science Confirms: Toxic Loops in the Womb

Science confirms that toxic loops begin early. As early as in the womb. Dr. Glover, prominent research in perinatal psychology, found that a mother's stress, anxiety, or trauma during pregnancy can significantly affect the development of the fetal brain. She confirms that the fetus' neurological system, especially the amygdala, the area responsible for emotional regulation, is wired and influenced in the womb. This increases the unborn child chances of *behavioral disorders later in life."* (Vivette Glover, *Journal of Child Psychology and Psychiatry* (2011)).

In other words, toxic mind loops can begin before a child ever speaks a word. A mother's unprocessed grief, generational fear, or unresolved trauma can be neurologically transferred to her unborn child creating **emotional imprints** that repeat through the child's internal narrative. This supports the reality that many people struggle with invisible thoughts, insecurities, or emotional triggers they can't trace because the root was planted in the womb.

My Lord! What Are We Doing to Our Babies in the Womb?

When we confront our internal scripts in adulthood phrases like *"I'm always afraid," "I don't belong," or "I sabotage everything I start"* it may not be rebellion or stubbornness, but a programmed loop that began as early as gestation. That's why deliverance and healing must include both spiritual authority and inner exploration, asking not just "what happened to me," but "what shaped me before I even knew myself?"

The good news? Jesus offers a reset, even for the mind loops we never consciously created. His power transcends time. Just like He told the man born blind that God's glory would be revealed in his healing, your story doesn't have to end with what was passed down—it can be rewritten by what is revealed. Having a safe and godly environment to give birth to a child is paramount to giving them a fighting chance of having godly thoughts.

From a spiritual standpoint, this aligns powerfully with Scriptures like Jeremiah 1:5: *"Before I formed you in the womb, I knew you..."* It reminds us that identity and destiny are established by God before birth, but the environment we are shaped in still plays a vital role in how that identity is perceived, received, or distorted. If a child is bathed in peace, love, and worship even in the womb it lays the foundation for a mindset of trust and security. If the womb is marked by stress, anger, or instability, those seeds can affect how the child later processes relationships, safety, or even their own self-worth. So yes, our thoughts can be shaped by experiences we have no memory of, because the mind begins forming long before words or logic. This means part of healing thought loops and replacing negative patterns may include acknowledging and releasing subconscious roots formed even in the womb through prayer, inner healing, and reestablishing identity in the truth of God's word. All these experiences become internal templates for how we understand the world and ourselves.

For example, a child who grows up in a household where affection is withheld may begin to associate love with performance. If they only receive praise when they get good grades or do chores, their young mind begins to think, *"I must earn love."* That belief becomes a foundational thought that can lead to perfectionism, people-pleasing, or fear of failure later in life. On the flip side, if a child witnesses frequent arguments, instability, or neglect, they may adopt internal scripts such as *"I can't trust anyone,"* or *"Chaos is normal."* These early experiences plant the seeds for the **thought loops** that develop into adult behaviors, reactions, and relational dynamics most often without us realizing where they started. The day we realized this truth is the day we can begin the process to health what happened before we remembered.

Prayer: To Heal The WOMB

This prayer reclaims the First Environment and heals the traumas that occurred in the womb.

Heavenly Father,

Thank You for forming me in my mother's womb and for knowing me before the foundations of the earth. Today, I invite You into the very beginning of my story. I ask You to enter the place where my heart first started to beat, where my identity began to form, and where early impressions were made before I ever had words.

If I was conceived in fear, rejection, or shame, I ask You to erase those impressions and replace them with Your truth: that I am loved, chosen, and fearfully made. If my mother or father struggled during the pregnancy, I forgive them now and release any unspoken pain I may still carry. Lord, I renounce every emotional imprint, every lie, every atmosphere of darkness that was transferred to me in the womb.

Wash me with Your love and truth. Heal my emotions at the root. Speak to the foundation of who I am and rebuild it with Your Word and Spirit. I break every assignment from the enemy that tried to shape my destiny before I could speak or choose.

Thank You, Lord, for healing what I don't even remember and restoring what I didn't know was broken. I receive wholeness in my beginnings, and I declare that I will live from a healed identity, in Jesus' name. Amen.

Tracing Pre-Memory Emotional Patterns

Tracing pre-memory emotional patterns helps to reflect on your birth story, journaling, activating the Holy Spirit's help and declaring what you want to happen in your life going forward.

[ACTIVITY 1: Tracing pre-memory emotional patterns](#) below is an exercise for you to perform recurring checkpoint in your healing journey. Revisit it when new emotional patterns emerge that don't seem to make sense. Remember, even what was once invisible can be uprooted, healed, and rewritten by the Spirit of God.

1.2.2 Influences Beyond the Home

Beyond the home, our culture, family systems, and environment also encode our belief systems. Culture tells us what is acceptable, valuable, or shameful. Sometimes in ways that conflict with our God-given identity. For example, a girl raised in a culture that prioritizes male success and silences female ambition may suppress her gifts, even in adulthood, believing thoughts like *"I shouldn't speak up"* or *"My success threatens others."* Likewise, family sayings like *"Money doesn't grow on trees"* or *"Don't trust anyone"* may seem harmless but create deep-rooted scarcity or suspicion mindsets. These repeated verbal affirmations become like **mental graffiti** etched into the soul until they are challenged. Neighborhoods marked by poverty, crime, or systemic injustice also reinforce subconscious thought systems like *"I'll never get out"* or *"This is just the way life is."* These cultural and environmental codes often go unchallenged, passed down like invisible blueprints for living until someone disrupts the narrative and chooses truth over tradition. Anyone can rise and **disrupt the narrative** of cultural, familial, and environmental influence and choose truth over tradition.

To disrupt the narrative of cultural, familial, and environmental influence means to recognize that not everything you were raised with is rooted in truth some of it was survival, dysfunction, fear, or simply misinformed tradition. From the language spoken over you to the silent rules you were taught to follow. Like, *"Don't question authority," "That's just how we do things," "Keep the family secrets,"* or *"Real men don't cry."* These norms become mental scripts that silently govern your life. The first step to disrupting this inherited narrative is awareness. You must ask: *Does this belief align with God's Word, or is it just what I was told? Does it empower me or imprison me?* This self-inquiry begins to uncover the hidden agreements you've made with dysfunction disguised as normalcy.

Disruption should come through intentional separation and truth-seeking but more often, it doesn't. Why? Because we, as humans, are naturally inclined toward:

Comfort over confrontation and

Familiarity over freedom.

Deep down, many of us know that certain patterns, beliefs, or environments are harmful but we also know that uprooting them will take effort, discomfort, and emotional excavation. And truthfully? Most people don't want to do that kind of work. It's not just laziness; it's fear, avoidance, and emotional fatigue disguised as passivity. Many of us don't enjoy the sobering and freeing fruits of disruption. Why? Because we as humans are inherently lazy. Many of us don't want to or take the time to do the work to disrupt the negative patterns in our lives that are causing these toxic thought cycles.

Disruption requires you to face the uncomfortable truths about where your patterns came from whether it's your culture, your parents, your past choices, or even your coping mechanisms. That's a level of vulnerability most people try to avoid. It's easier to say, *"That's just how I am"* than to say, *"This version of me was shaped by pain, and I need to change it."* Doing the work means grieving what you never got, confronting what you've been tolerating, and releasing identities you've outgrown and that's no small task. So instead, people often stay stuck in cycles, waiting for disruption to come **by force or osmosis.** But most often, disruption comes through crisis, burnout, betrayal, breakdown, prolong sickness, at deaths door or God's divine interruption rather than initiating it through intentional truth-seeking and soul work. But here's the sobering truth:

If you don't disrupt the pattern,

The pattern will eventually disrupt you.

God, in HIS mercy, will allow pressure to build until

you're forced to face what you tried to ignore. Not to punish you, but to free you. The cost of passivity is always higher than the cost of obedience. So, if you want true transformation, you must do more than notice the pattern. You must be *willing* to confront it, challenge it, and **do the work to break it**. Even when it's uncomfortable, inconvenient, or unfamiliar. That's where healing starts. That's where legacy changes.

Disruption comes through intentional separation and truth-seeking. It might mean distancing yourself emotionally from certain cultural mindsets that glorify brokenness or pride themselves on silence and secrecy. For example, if your culture normalizes overworking as a badge of honor, but God calls you into rest and balance (Matthew 11:28), then you must confront and reject the hustle mindset. If your family taught you that vulnerability is weakness, but Scripture calls us to confess, heal, and walk in the light (James 5:16), then you must choose truth over loyalty to brokenness.

This process isn't easy. It may involve feeling like the "black sheep," confronting generational patterns, or enduring misunderstanding from those still bound to the old narrative. But Jesus Himself said in *Mark 7:13* that tradition can "make the word of God of no effect." Disrupting tradition is about restoring truth to its rightful place. It's declaring,

"Just because it's familiar doesn't mean it's healthy."

"Just because it's cultural doesn't mean it's spiritual."

You begin building a new foundation by renewing your mind (Romans 12:2), surrounding yourself with truth-tellers, and creating an environment that reinforces your healing whether that's through books, mentorship, therapy, or spiritual community.

Ultimately, choosing truth over tradition is choosing **freedom over familiarity**, even when familiarity feels safe. It is saying, *"This end with me."* And when you do that, you don't just set yourself free, you break the mold for everyone who comes after you.

Here's a **powerful declaration and prayer** designed to break cultural and familial cycles that no longer align with God's truth, and to establish new patterns rooted in identity, freedom, and legacy.

DECLARATION: Break Cultural and Family Cycles

I declare that I am no longer bound to any cultural, familial, or environmental tradition that conflicts with the truth of God's Word. I am not a prisoner of patterns. I am a product of purpose. Every lie I believed, every silent agreement I made, and every generational mindset that tried to limit me is now broken by the authority of Jesus

Christ.

I am a bloodline breaker.

I am the standard raiser.

I choose truth over tradition, healing over habit, and wholeness over history. I speak to every inherited cycle whether spoken or unspoken and I say: **you end with me.** *From this moment forward, I align my thoughts, words, and actions with the truth of God's Word. I declare freedom over my mind, my emotions, my decisions, and my descendants. In Jesus' name, I walk in generational restoration, restitution and legacy alignment. Amen.*

Prayer: Renounce Old Patterns

Dear Heavenly Father,

Thank You for revealing to me the patterns, beliefs, and traditions that have shaped my thinking and behavior. Today, I come before You not with blame, but with boldness ready to surrender every cultural mindset and family cycle that does not reflect Your will for my life.

I repent for any agreements I have made with fear, pride, silence, performance, poverty, manipulation, emotional neglect, or any belief that contradicts the truth of who You've called me to be. I renounce every spoken word, family expectation, cultural pressure, and generational stronghold that has kept me bound.

I break the power of these patterns in Jesus' name. I cancel every spiritual agreement tied to my bloodline that leads to cycles of dysfunction, limitation, or spiritual blindness. I invite Your truth to replace every lie. Rewire my thoughts. Renew my mind. Restore my emotional DNA. Teach me how to live in freedom and to build a new legacy for those who come after me.

Holy Spirit, I ask for discernment to identify subtle patterns, strength to walk in truth, and courage to be different even if I must walk alone for a season. Let my healing be the beginning of generational transformation. I declare that I am free, and I walk boldly into the destiny You've written for me. In Jesus, PRECIOUS and POWERFUL Name, AMEN.

1.2.3 PATHOLOGY: Genetics Inheritance

Pathology refers to the emotional and psychological **"wounds and wiring"** that can be inherited or developed over time. Trauma whether sudden or chronic can permanently alter the brain's wiring and create defense mechanisms that masquerade as personality traits. For example, a person who experienced betrayal in a key relationship may begin to think *"People always leave,"* causing them to sabotage future connections before they even begin. These aren't just thoughts they're protection systems developed by the brain and soul to avoid re-experiencing pain.

On a deeper level, genetic predispositions to anxiety, depression, or impulsiveness can also shape how a person interprets events and relationships. Even more complex is the emerging field of **epigenetics**, which suggests that **trauma experienced by one generation can chemically alter the DNA of the next.** Meaning a person may feel fear or emotional tension without any clear source. When left unhealed, these inherited patterns become **invisible instructions** that shape how someone sees the world and interacts within it. But when recognized and surrendered to God, these can be healed and rewritten through spiritual and therapeutic renewal.

EPIGENETICS: How Genes Work

Your **genes** are like instructions inside your body that tell them how to grow, what color your eyes will be, how tall you might be, or **even how your body reacts to stress.** You get these genes from your parents. Half from your mom, and half from your dad. This tells us that we are intrinsically tied to our parents, thus, our ancestors. So, even if you don't know your parents, let's say they died before you really got to know them or live with them or you were adopted, you will never escape them. WHY? Because their DNA is passed down in your genes. That is why it is usually referred to as our BLOODLINE. We can trace it all the way back to the Garden of Eden, after Adam and Eve sin. The bible said that they were immediately saw their nakedness. They immediately recognize that they no longer had the Glory of God covering them. Then the bible goes on to say that they were AFRAID. Now fear has entered our bloodline. But guess what? No need to fear. God NEVER meant for us to be this way. We can change our bloodline. If you want a different outcome or different response system WE MUST get a new bloodline.

Here's another cool part about genes. **Genes are like light switches**. They don't always turn "on" or "off" by themselves. What you eat, how you feel, how much sleep you get, and even how much love or stress you experience can flip those switches. This is where **epigenetics** comes in.

Epigenetics is like the **remote control** for your genes. It doesn't change the actual instructions (the DNA), but it controls **how and when** those instructions get used. So even though your DNA doesn't change, the way your body reads and reacts to it can change, especially during big life events or when someone goes through trauma or stress.

Let's say you have a gene that's like a recipe for

making "calm feelings." But when someone is under a lot of stress like being yelled at a lot, feeling unsafe, or being really scared the body can add chemicals to that gene that tell it: *"Don't cook that calm recipe right now."* So, the gene is still there, but it's not doing its job the same way anymore. This is called chemical tagging, and it affects how your body responds sometimes for a long time.

One of the most famous studies on this topic comes from researchers **Meaney and Szyf (2004)**. In this study, scientists looked at how baby rats acted differently depending on how much their moms took care of them. Baby rats that got lots of licking and grooming from their moms had genes that helped them stay calm and handle stress better. But the baby rats whose moms didn't take care of them as much had more trouble with stress and here's the big deal.

Their stress genes were chemically changed.

The researchers found that the difference wasn't in the DNA itself, but in how those genes were turned on or off using little chemical markers. This showed that how you're treated can affect how your genes behave even without changing the genes themselves. And these changes could last their whole lives! So, when we say trauma can be passed down, it doesn't mean your

DNA is broken. It means that the "switches" on your DNA can get stuck in the wrong position but with love, safety, therapy, and healing, those switches can be turned back on again. But most of all, living a godly live in Christ can rewire your gene switches. God and science agree, your story can be rewritten.

Breaking Negative Inherited 'Epigenetics'

First, we must inquire about our specific family iniquity and Generational Patterns. Some family's iniquity is rooted in PRIDE, others, WRATH, ENVY, PERVERSION. MURDER, etc. It behooves us to do a spiritual ancestral trace and find out. We really don't have to look to far. We just have to examine our own life patterns, then those of our siblings, our parents, Aunties and Cousins, Grandparents. If you are still clueless JUST ASK. Someone is still alive that can tell you what's up.

In spiritual language, this aligns with the biblical concept of iniquity the twisted patterns passed down through bloodlines (Exodus 34:7, "...visiting the iniquity of the fathers upon the children"). Iniquity is not just sin it's a spiritual distortion in the lineage that needs to be healed and reset.

The good news is God can heal what was inherited, just like He can redeem what was chosen. The same God who said, *"Behold, I make all things new"* (Revelation 21:5) can rewrite the biological and spiritual imprint that trauma has left on your life.

Identifying 'Real Life' Epigenetic Influence

1. **FEAR WITHOUT CAUSE:**
   A young woman experiences anxiety every time someone leaves her life even in small ways like a friend canceling a lunch date. She has no major abandonment wounds in her personal story. But when she learns her grandmother was left to raise four children alone after being abandoned by her husband, it begins to make sense. That trauma may have programmed her DNA to brace for loss, even when there's no immediate threat.

2. **Emotional Numbness or Avoidance**
   A man has trouble crying, connecting, or expressing love—even to his spouse or children. He feels guilt for not "feeling deeply," but can't access what's wrong. Upon further exploration, he learns that his father served in war and never processed the trauma, eventually becoming emotionally closed off. The son may have inherited a survival pattern, where emotional distance was a protection mechanism.

3. **Poverty or Scarcity Mindset**
   A businesswoman consistently undercharges or sabotages her success, even though she's qualified and

competent.

Her family history includes generations of poverty and systemic exclusion. Though she has "escaped" the environment, her nervous system is still operating on scarcity-mode, fearing that security is temporary or unearned.

Healing Epigenetic Trauma

The healing of Epigenetics trauma must be done through God and Therapy lead by born-again, spirit lead therapist or counselors. WHY? Spiritual healing is a crucial distinction that speaks to the depth of true healing, especially when dealing with epigenetic trauma, which reaches into both the soul and the body, the seen and unseen, the generational and the spiritual. If not done correctly what was meant to free us will ultimately damage

The study of **epigenetics** has revolutionized how we understand the impact of trauma not just on individuals, but on entire generations. Unlike changes to DNA's genetic code itself, epigenetics refers to how behaviors and environment can cause changes that affect the way genes work. Traumatic experiences such as war, abuse, poverty, neglect, or systemic oppression can **chemically alter the expression of genes**, and these changes can be passed down through generations. In simple terms, *pain can be inherited.* This is why

Epigenetic Trauma Must Be Healed Through God *and* Spirit-Led Therapy

Epigenetic Trauma Is Both Physical and Spiritual. Epigenetic trauma doesn't just live in your mind, it's **encoded in your biology**, buried in your nervous system, and passed down through emotional behaviors. At the same time, it's deeply **spiritual** because much of what's inherited isn't just stress. It's **generational iniquity**, emotional strongholds, and spiritual assignments passed down through bloodlines.

Healing that reaches both realms

Science alone can help you understand *how* trauma affects your genes. Therapy alone can help you process the trauma and reframe your story. But only God, through the Holy Spirit, can go back to the womb of generations, break spiritual covenants, heal emotional wounds you don't even remember, and reset what was encoded before you had language. That's why this work requires both the revelation of God and the training of therapy a marriage of truth and technique.

In addition, **spiritual Patterns Hide Behind Psychological Symptoms.** A born-again, Spirit-led therapist doesn't just see your pain as a diagnosis, they see it as an assignment from the enemy that must be dismantled. While secular counselors can guide you to helpful cognitive tools, they may not recognize when a generational spirit of rejection, fear, or addiction is manifesting. They may explain your anxiety, but not the demonic cycle behind it. They themselves are also bound by their own negative generational epigenetics so their knowledge is limited and only exists in the physical realm. Only what they learn in school and not the Holy Spirit.

A Spirit-led counselor will:

- Help you walk through **inner healing** and **deliverance** alongside therapeutic tools
- Teach you how to **renounce spiritual agreements**, not just manage symptoms
- Invite the **Holy Spirit** into the session for revelation, discernment, and freedom
- Use professional knowledge while also leading you into the presence of God

"Where the Spirit of the Lord is, there is freedom." – 2 Corinthians 3:17. So, healing Requires Identity, Not Just Insight.

Secular therapy might help you understand your past, but it often cannot give you a new identity. It may help you cope, but it cannot give you a renewed mind or a redeemed purpose. Epigenetic trauma often leaves people asking: *"Why do I feel broken and disconnected?"* The answer lies not just in psychology, but in identity restoration knowing *who you are in Christ*, and what God says about you.

A Spirit-led therapist will remind you:

- You are not your trauma.
- You are not your family's dysfunction.
- You are not cursed, you are **chosen**.
- You can break any and all curses through Christ.
- You are a new creation (2 Corinthians 5:17), and the healing of your DNA starts with the blood of Jesus.

The Holy Spirit Can Access What the Mind Cannot.

Therapy helps uncover memories. God can reveal the ones you never knew you needed healing from. Therapy helps you speak. God helps you weep, surrender, and be restored. Where trauma has written a story of pain, the Holy Spirit becomes the Editor-in-Chief, rewriting your narrative not just on paper, but in your cells, your soul, and your spirit. The healing of epigenetic trauma is not just about breaking cycles, it's about breaking spiritual bondage, releasing emotional residue, and resetting generational identity. That's why you need ...

Jesus as the Healer

The Holy Spirit as the Revealer, And...

A Spirit-filled therapist or counselor as Guider

Together, they walk with you to reclaim what was stolen, restore what was broken, and redeem what was hidden. What's more sobering is that these inherited emotional codes don't always come with a label. You may feel persistent fear, shame, anxiety, or emotional heaviness without a specific experience to trace it to. That's because you may be carrying the echo of someone else's trauma a grandparent who survived racism, a parent who lost a child, or a lineage marked by abandonment or grief. These become **invisible instructions** encoded into your soul: *"Don't trust," "Always protect yourself," "Something bad is going to happen," "You're alone."*

Passing Down Good Epigenetics

While much of the conversation around epigenetics focuses on the negative trauma, stress, and dysfunction it's important to know that positive, life-giving experiences and spiritual alignment can also be passed down through epigenetic influence. Just as trauma can "tag" genes and impact future generations, so can love, peace, safety, joy, and spiritual devotion. Here is [EXERCISE 2: Passing Down Good Epigenetics.](#)

Biblical Foundation - Generational Blessing Is Real

Scripture confirms this truth long before science did. ***Exodus 20:6(NIV)*** : says *"But showing love to a thousand generations of those who love me and keep my commandments."* This is **spiritual epigenetics** in action. God honors not just your personal walk with Him but the legacy it creates in your DNA, your children, and their children. When a parent or grandparent lives a Christ-centered, Spirit-filled life, they are literally laying down a blueprint of righteousness, peace, and purpose in their bloodline. Epigenetic research and published studies confirm the connections between the scientific and the biology of blessings.

Epigenetic studies have shown that when individuals are exposed to nurturing, calm, and spiritually grounded environments, their bodies produce:

- **Less cortisol** (stress hormone)
- **More oxytocin** (bonding/love hormone)
- **Greater resilience to stress**
- **More adaptive emotional regulation**

These chemical patterns affect gene expression and can be inherited by children, creating an emotional and neurological baseline of security, compassion, faith, and balance. If a child grows up hearing scripture and prayer, watching their parent forgive and walk in peace, experiencing worship and emotional stability and witnessing faith in action under pressure…they are being **spiritually and neurologically programmed** for peace, faith, and favor even before they understand what those words mean.

This reminds me of the scripture that says, train up a child in the way that they should go and when they are old they will not depart [scripture]. This shows that God also recognize the power of environments and gave man a solution to combat generating negative patterns in their offsprings. Today we see grownups with certain behaviors that can be traced back to the way they were trained.

Here is an example of spiritual neurological programmed life: *A young person may not understand why they has a natural inclination to worship, why they values honesty, or why they instinctively turn to God in moments of stress until they realize that their grandparent was a prayer warrior who covered them while they were in the womb. Their worship became an atmospheric code for his inner world. Their grandparents' declarations became a prophetic canopy that shaped their resilience.*

Passing down good epigenetics is as real as passing down negativity in the genes. When we live a Spirit-led life, we don't just bless our own timeline we secure our own BLOODLINE. You build a legacy of favor, identity, and divine alignment for generations you may never meet. Your obedience today becomes their instinct tomorrow. Your healed voice becomes their first truth. Your worship becomes their blueprint, and your surrender becomes their security.

Surrendering Inherited Patterns for Healing

Here's a spiritual and therapeutic [EXERCISE 3: to surrender, heal, and rewrite]() what was passed down

Declaration: Healing Generational Trauma

"Father, I surrender every hidden trauma—known and unknown, mine and inherited. I no longer carry what You died to break. I place my history, my family, and my DNA under the blood of Jesus. I speak to every memory encoded in my body, every fear lodged in my soul, and every pattern wired in my brain, and I say: be healed. I welcome Your truth, Your Spirit, and Your blueprint for my identity and my future. Let healing begin in me and flow through me for generations to come. Amen."

And while our lifestyle, habits, and spiritual alignment shape the environments we pass down, one of the most powerful tools in this process is often the most overlooked is **our self-talk**. What we speak to ourselves silently is just as influential as what we say over our children or environment out loud. The internal dialogue we rehearse daily becomes part of the atmosphere we live in and by extension, the emotional climate we create for those around us. If we want to pass on peace, confidence, and faith, we must first model those qualities in how we speak to ourselves. Self-talk is a seed. What you repeatedly tell yourself. Whether "I'm never enough" or "I am who God says I am" not only shapes your behavior but can also become part of the invisible code your descendants inherit. That's why the legacy of healing begins in your inner voice. To pass on blessing, we must first align our inner conversation with truth. The self-talk we engage in, especially during emotionally heightened moments when we're happy, sad, angry, betrayed, or disappointed. All this leads to **Emotional Self-Talk:**

Emotional self-talk is what we tell ourselves in moments of Intensity. Emotional self-talk is one of the most overlooked, yet deeply influential, sources of our thought patterns. **Self-talk** is what we engage in during emotional highs and lows. In moments of celebration or crisis, the internal dialogue we choose can either reinforce truth or perpetuate lies. For instance, when someone is overlooked for a promotion, they may think, *"I'll never be good enough,"* or *"No one sees my value."* In a moment of heartbreak, one might internally declare, *"I must not be lovable,"* or *"I'm always the one left behind."* These thoughts, though fueled by emotion, become internal decrees that, if unchallenged, solidify into beliefs. On the flip side, even positive moments can reveal faulty wiring for example, someone receiving praise may think, *"I better not mess up next time,"* revealing a performance-based identity. Over time, these emotional echoes form loops: we rehearse the same toxic phrases, deepen the grooves of self-doubt, and set spiritual agreements in motion without realizing it.

Proverbs 18:21 says, *"Death and life are in the power of the tongue,"* and that includes the tongue of our internal dialogue. What we tell ourselves during joy, pain, anger, or grief becomes the subconscious foundation of our future decisions, relationships, and self-worth until we consciously interrupt that voice, interrogate its truth, and replace it with God's word and perspective. These internal dialogues *"I'll never be good enough," "Everyone leaves,"* and *"I don't need anyone,"* becomes mantras that reinforce mental loops. Over time, these sources craft an internal narrative that produces thoughts, which flow seamlessly into our words, and ultimately shape our actions.

This is the invisible loop: *Thoughts → Words → Actions.* And until we identify and disrupt the sources feeding our thoughts, we will continue to repeat patterns that seem like personal choices but are subconscious scripts written by life's unhealed wounds. God doesn't just want to hear what we think. God wants to heal *why* we think it. Only then can we break the loop and replace it with a divine thought cycle aligned with truth, identity, and purpose.

TRAINING YOUR INNER VOICE

Training our inner voice shapes Self-Talk for Generational Impact. What we speak to ourselves silently is just as influential as what we speak over our children or environment out loud. The internal dialogue we rehearse daily becomes part of the atmosphere we live in and by extension, the emotional climate we create for those around us.

If we want to pass on peace, confidence, and faith, we must first model those qualities in how we speak to ourselves. Self-talk is a seed. What you repeatedly tell yourself whether "I'm never enough" or "I am who God says I am" not only shapes your behavior but can also become part of the invisible code your descendants inherit. That's why the legacy of healing begins in your inner voice. To pass on blessing, we must first align our inner conversation with truth.

Start each day by listening to your internal language:
- Is it filled with fear, doubt, or self-condemnation?

- Or is it infused with grace, truth, and divine identity?

The more you train your inner voice to echo God's Word, the more you program your mind and your legacy to live from a healed, whole, and Spirit-led place. Once your mind is trained then your mouth will say what's in the heart and your fingers will automatically follow by typing and texting the words from your thoughts. The bible says, "A good man out of the good treasure of his heart brings forth good; and an evil man out of the evil treasure of his heart brings forth evil. For out of the abundance of the heart his mouth speaks." (*Luke 6:45 NKJV*). This verse beautifully affirms the connection between what we store internally (our thoughts, emotions, beliefs) and what eventually comes out in our words. It's a key foundational truth for *DELETE TH@T*, especially in helping readers understand why renewing the heart and mind is essential before rewriting language.

Toxic thought loops operate like invisible chains binding us to false beliefs, distorted identity, and emotional cycles that feel natural but are nurtured by unhealed pain. These loops often form quietly, through early life experiences, unspoken expectations, or repeated emotional wounds. Whether rooted in trauma, culture, or inherited emotional memory, toxic thoughts do more than affect our mindset. They become the blueprint for how we show up in life. We learned that recognizing and renewing these loops is the first step to true transformation. By bringing our thought patterns into the light of truth and surrendering them to God, we begin to break the cycle of silent sabotage and invite healing at the root level.

But thoughts don't stay hidden forever. What we meditate on in private will eventually manifest in public through our words. The mouth becomes the microphone of the mind, often revealing the very patterns we claim to be free from. In the next section, we'll examine how self-sabotaging speech reinforces the toxic loops we just uncovered—and how learning to delete those declarations is key to rewriting your inner narrative.

1.3 SELF-SABOTAGING SPEECH (MOUTH)

If toxic thoughts are the seeds, then our **words are the water** that determine whether those seeds die or grow. Our thoughts don't stay silent, they look for expression. And often, that expression flows straight out of our mouths. What we mutter in frustration, joke about in pain, or repeat out of habit may feel harmless, but spiritually...

Every word is an agreement

With either heaven or with hell.

That brings us to the mouth. Our words are not fillers. They are fuel. What we say becomes a decree in the spirit. When we say things like "I don't have" or "I can't," we aren't just venting we're inviting. These statements carry weight in the unseen realm and can serve as spiritual demands for demonic manifestation. Scripture tells us in Proverbs 18:21, "Death and life are in the power of the tongue." What you speak sets your atmosphere and gives permission to either darkness or light.

Mouth: Microphone to the Spirit Realm

Every syllable we speak either stirs up life or summons death. This is not poetic exaggeration; it's spiritual law. We speak one of two things, LIFE or DEATH. In many cases, we often speak more DEATH than LIFE. It is like DEATH is a natural and automatic. Meaning the mouth holds more than expression, it holds permission. What we say becomes a decree in the spirit. When we speak things like *"I can't," "I'll never," "I'm broke,"* or *"Nobody wants me,"* we aren't just venting we're inviting. These are spiritual invitations, unspoken contracts that give demonic forces access to manifest what we've declared. Demons don't need full rituals to move they just need your agreement.

Words like *"I don't have"* may feel like facts, but when spoken repeatedly, they program your atmosphere and reinforce a cycle of lack. Words like *"I'm just like my mother"* or *"It always happens this way"* may seem like observations, but they often reflect internal vows you didn't realize you made. These kinds of phrases reinforce toxic thought loops and create emotional atmospheres of despair, fear, or unworthiness not just around you, but within you.

Spiritually, your mouth functions like a governor's pen. What you speak becomes a policy in your inner world. It determines what kind of atmosphere you live in, what kind of warfare you attract, and what kind of freedom you forfeit. God created the world with words and since you're made in His image, **so do you**. What you declare becomes the architecture of your life. The enemy knows this, which is why he works hard to influence your speech. Because if he can hijack your mouth, he can help build a life you don't want **using your own words as blueprints**.

That's why self-sabotaging speech is not just about being negative, and positive speech shouldn't be taken lightly. They are both **prophetic**. It's about taking back the authority of your voice and aligning your speech with truth, identity, and destiny. Because once your mouth is delivered, your environment must follow.

Declaration: "I Take Back My Voice"

I take back the power of my voice and repent for every word I've spoken that agreed with failure or lack. I break every cycle that my mouth has reinforced, and I cancel every curse that I've placed over my own life. I cancel every careless word, every self-cursing phrase, and every lie I've spoken over myself. My words will no longer serve fear, shame, or defeat. I declare that my mouth is a vessel of life, not death. My words are aligned with truth, soaked in grace, and filled with power. I speak life into my identity, my future, and my legacy. I speak healing, favor, and breakthrough into my atmosphere. I prophesy over myself:

I am not cursed, I am covered.

I am not limited, I am led.

I am called, I am capable,

And I am becoming who God says I am

My mouth is no longer a tool of sabotage

My words are a sword of victory.

I will speak what heaven says until my life looks like heaven's blueprint. In Jesus' name, I reclaim the sound of victory in my speech. Amen.

Here are links to two powerful activities 'below' to activate speech transformation.

[ACTIVITY 4: DELETE TH@T" Language Checklist](#)

[EXERCISE 5: 7 days Anti-Self-Sabotage](#)

Reminder: The goal is not perfection it's awareness, repentance, and reset.

If our thoughts are the blueprint and our words are the decree, then our actions become the construction site where patterns are built, lived, and reinforced. After all, it's not just what we think or say that shapes our lives, it's what we consistently *do*. You can think healed thoughts and speak life-giving words, but if your daily movement still reflects old patterns, your progress will be stalled by contradiction. That's why the final and most visible layer of the toxic loop is our behavior the choices, habits, routines, and reactions that quietly tell the truth about what we really believe. In the next section, we'll examine how behavioral cycles often operate beneath awareness, and how breaking free from movement that mirrors bondage is essential to walking in full alignment with the freedom you're confessing.

1.4 BEHAVIORAL CYCLES (MOVEMENT)

Movement is proof of belief. What you repeatedly do

reveals what you truly believe no matter what you say or intend. Behavioral cycles are the lived-out expressions of internal agreements. They're the patterns you walk in every day, often without realizing they're echoing unhealed places, unconscious vows, or generational dysfunction. For example, you may say you're ready for healthy love but keep pursuing emotionally unavailable people. You may declare financial breakthroughs but continually sabotage budgeting or overspend to soothe stress. These aren't just habits, their emotional faults, often formed by years of survival, fear, or identity confusion. If left unchallenged, these cycles become silent architects of stagnation, making you feel stuck—not because change isn't available, but because your feet are still following a familiar script. So, how does one begin the process of recognizing, confronting, and rerouting the movements so that their life can finally reflect the healing that began in your mind and ended up in your mouth.

The rerouting of movement that is what you repeatedly do becomes your rhythm, your routine, your reality is manifest daily in our behavior / actions. The way you behave, respond, avoid, or act out are all expressions of what you've been thinking and saying.

Our habits are simply thoughts wearing shoes.

You can't change your life without changing your behavior, and you can't change your behavior until you confront the thoughts and words that built it.

Your Habits Are Thoughts Wearing Shoes

Now let's take it a step further and examine our movement. This is where everything you think and say begins to take form in the physical realm. Your movement is what confirms or contradicts your declarations. You can say all the right things, even believe the truth intellectually, but your daily actions will always expose your actual alignment. The way you move through life, how you walk into a room, how you follow through on commitments, how you handle conflict or avoid confrontation these are all embodied extensions of your internal programming. Movement is the visible footprint of your invisible agreements.

What You Repeatedly Do Becomes Your Rhythm, Your Routine, Your Reality. Repetition becomes rhythm. Rhythm becomes routine. Routine becomes reality. Every behavior you practice becomes easier to repeat the next time, good or bad.

Science calls this neural wiring.

Scripture calls it habitual living.

If you repeatedly procrastinate, isolate, or lash out, that behavior solidifies into a rhythm that feels "normal" even if it's destructive. Eventually, you're not just reacting you're living in auto-pilot mode, unknowingly scripting your life around your habits. And here's the danger. Most people don't question their rhythm until it creates a crisis. But the truth is, every repeated behavior is either building your future or blocking it. And since movement determines direction, your behavior is not just a reflection of your life, it's setting the course for where you're going. You see, behavior Is the Echo of Thoughts and Words.

Every choice you make, every reaction you display, every decision you delay is tied to a mental narrative and verbal agreement that came first. Behavior is rarely random. It's a response to what you've been meditating on and verbalizing, even subconsciously. If you avoid opportunities, it may be because you've thought, *"I'm not qualified,"* and said, *"I'll probably fail."* If you isolate in relationships, it could be the byproduct of a thought like, *"People always leave,"* reinforced by phrases like, *"I'm better off alone."* These thoughts and words create a behavioral loop that becomes hard to escape until the source is exposed and corrected. This is why Scripture constantly pairs belief with action because right thinking and speaking must ultimately translate into right living. You Can't Change Your Life Without Changing Your Behavior. Wanting change is not the same as creating it. Many people pray for transformation but never address their behavioral patterns.

Many speak deliverance but walk in dysfunction.

Why? Because changing your life requires a decision that goes beyond desire it requires discipline, disruption, and new direction. You can't live in healing while walking out of the same old habits. You can't speak wholeness while your actions reflect brokenness. The bible is very clear on this matter via **2 Corinthians 4:16 (KJV)** that says: *"Though our outward man perish, yet the inward man is renewed day by day."* **2 Corinthians 4:16** becomes deeply relevant and powerful when held up against the reality expressed in the dichotomy in what our mouths say and our movements. The difference between the perishing on the outward man while the inward man is being renewed daily point to an intentional and deliberate effort to separate spiritual renewal from surface routine.

The Apostle Paul is credited as the writer of the book of Corinthians and in 2 Corinthians 4:16 he describes a divine paradox of Spiritual Renewal vs. Surface Routine. This is our external selves (our bodies, behaviors, and old patterns) are naturally wearing down, but the inward man the core of our identity, spirit, and beliefs can be renewed daily through intimacy with God. But here's the key:

Inward renewal isn't automatic

Just because you say spiritual things. It requires consistent engagement, surrender, and discipline.

Many people say the right words "I'm delivered," "I'm healed," "I'm moving on" but still live bound to old movement patterns. Why? Because *true renewal happens from the inside out*, not outside in. You can dress up outside and still feel spiritually decayed. You can shout freedom in public and still be secretly bound in private. Paul reminds us that although the "outward man" may be weak, failing, or stuck in habit, the inner man can be rebuilt daily if we're willing to show up for the internal work. Rebuilding daily internal habits is done through discipline, disruption and redirection.

Discipline, Disruption, and Direction matters because speaking deliverance is the first step but walking in it requires:

- **Discipline** to renew your mind daily (Romans 12:2)
- **Disruption** to break patterns your body and brain have grown used to
- **New direction** to move differently, even when the old route feels familiar

You can't say *"I'm healed"* and still live in patterns of brokenness. That's not transformation, that's contradiction. What Paul is offering is a reminder that internal renewal is daily, intentional, and spiritual. It happens through relationship, truth, and the Holy

Spirit not willpower alone. So, What's the Connection?

2 Corinthians 4:16 also shows us that change starts inward, and the inner man must be renewed day by day to align with the truth you're declaring. If your mouth says *deliverance*, but your movement still mimics dysfunction, the issue isn't your intention, it's your inner man's daily neglect. The soul and spirit must be constantly realigned with heaven's truth so that your actions eventually match your declarations. The outward man perishes habits, reflexes, emotional reactions but the inward man is where transformation begins. If you want new movements, new outcomes, and lasting breakthroughs, your healing must be fed daily just like your body.

Until you bring your behavior into submission with your declarations, your words will always sound good, but your life will remain unchanged. Real transformation happens when movement matches the mindset. And movement is how we act, our behavioral changes. And we can't change our behavior until we confront the thoughts and words that built it. Trying to change behavior without addressing the belief that building it is like repainting a house with a cracked foundation. You'll look better for a while, but eventually, everything will collapse under pressure. That's why behavioral change must begin with a confrontation of truth. What belief created this behavior? What lies are you agreeing with every time you make this choice? What thought justified the habit? What words have kept it alive? Until you answer those questions, you'll keep treating symptoms instead of pulling up the root. But when you trace the behavior to its origin and replace the lie with truth you don't just change your routine. You rewire your reality.

Behavioral Cycles & Movement

Identifying Behavioral Cycles (Movement) will help you reflect, apply, and spiritually engage with the revelations on a personal level. You will be able to identify repeated behaviors, emotional triggers, and patterns that contradict your declarations or divine identity. Here is the link to the Behavioral Cycles / Movement exercise below

[ACTIVITY 6: Behavioral Cycles & Movement worksheet](#)

[EXERCISE 7: Behavior vs Beliefs Alignment](#)

Prayer: Thoughts → Words → Movement

Heavenly, Father,

Today, I surrender my movements, my habits, my cycles, and my reactions. I admit that some of the things I've been doing are not aligned with the healing I've been praying for or the truth I've been speaking.

Lord, I ask You to help me identify the thoughts that built these behaviors, and the words that reinforced them. Give me the grace to trace the pattern, the courage to confront it, and the power to change it. I no longer want to walk in contradiction I want to walk in alignment.

I speak over my body, my routine, my choices, and my reactions: *You will line up with truth. You will reflect the freedom I have in Christ. You will obey the voice of the Lord. I am not bound by my history. I am free to walk in new habits, healed movement, and divine rhythm.*

Let my life preach louder than my words. Let my steps confirm what I believe. Let my behavior glorify the One who is renewing me from the inside out.

In Jesus' name, amen.

Please understand this, writing is never random. It is a DECREE and has roots. Whether it is these exercises or it's a journal entry, a text message, or a social media post, what you write flows from what you think and speak. And in the spirit realm, writing carries legal authority. It becomes a policy. A public decree. A governing law. When you write from a broken belief, you codify that brokenness into your reality. That's why deleting isn't just mental, it's spiritual warfare.

When we casually or emotionally write statements

like "I'll never get ahead," or "I don't have enough," we're unknowingly placing demands in the spirit for lack to manifest. These words are agreements. And spiritual laws respond to agreements. The power to bind and loose begins in thought but is executed through the spoken and written words.

Once you've recognized that your behavior reflects your beliefs, it's important to understand how those beliefs were formed and why they carry so much power. Thoughts become words, and words become action but when you write those words down, something shifts. The written word doesn't just express belief, it enforces it. Writing is not just reflection, it's legislation. In the spiritual realm, your written words function as decrees, shaping the policy of your life. That's why Scripture tells us to *"write the vision and make it plain"* (Habakkuk 2:2) because what's written becomes official.

Which brings us to a deeper truth: your soul operates like a government. Every thought is a policy proposal. Every word is a public address. Every behavior is the law in action. And what you write, well, that's a formal decree. A written law that your life spiritually and emotionally is expected to follow. To fully uproot dysfunction and enforce wholeness, we must begin to govern our internal world the same way a righteous kingdom would through intentional leadership, divine laws, and surrender authority. Our surrendered authority from our written decrees is seen in the spirit as the **'GOVERNING OF OUR SOUL.'**

1.5 GOVERNMING ANOLOGY OF THE SOUL

Imagine your soul as a city, and your mind, mouth, and movement as the three branches of internal government. Your mind is the legislative branch, crafting thoughts and perspectives. Your mouth is the executive branch, announcing and enforcing those thoughts. And your movement, your actions and habits is the judicial branch, interpreting and living out the law that was passed. Now, think of your written words, your journals, notes, posts, and declarations as official legislation. Once written, they hold power in both the spiritual and natural realms. Proverbs 25:28 says, *"He that hath no rule over his own spirit is like a city broken down, and without walls."* Without intentional self-governance, we become vulnerable to invasion of lies, dysfunction, and demonic influence. Understanding is key to recognizing who's truly ruling your internal government and how to enforce new decrees that align with heaven's constitution for your life.

Think of your inner life as a spiritual government. Your mind is the cabinet that drafts thoughts and beliefs. Your mouth is the press secretary making public announcements, and your movement, your body is the military or enforcement arm carrying out the decrees. If the mind is toxic, the cabinet is corrupted. If the mouth speaks negativity, the policies are flawed. And if the actions follow suit, your entire government, the way your life is run is in chaos. Proverbs 25:28 gives a perfect picture: "He that hath no rule over his own spirit is like a city that is broken down, and without walls." It's time to govern your life with wisdom, order, and authority. Here is how soul governing statements work.

SOUL GOVERNMENT STATMENTS

- **Mind (Legislative Branch):** Proposes internal policy through thought life. Formulates ideas, perspectives, and worldviews.

- **Mouth (Executive Branch):** Declares those policies aloud, giving voice and authority to what is believed.

- **Movement (Judicial Branch):** Lives out and interprets those thoughts and words in action, habit, and routine.

- **Written Word (Official Decree):** Finalizes and formalizes what you think, say, and live. Becomes law until intentionally revised.

SOUL GOVERNMENT PICTORAL DIAGRAM

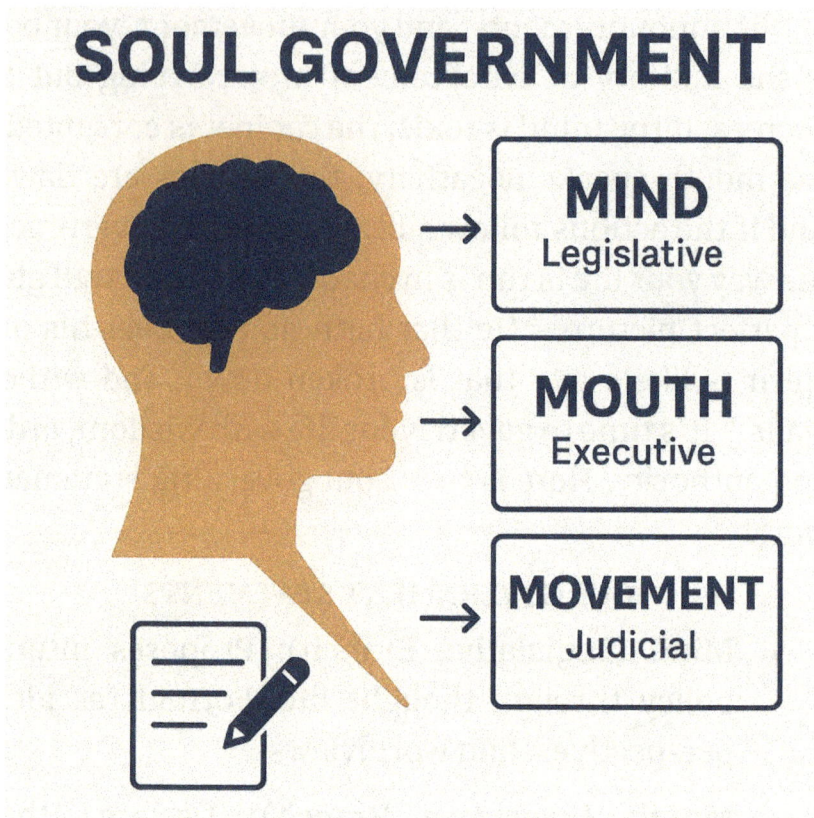

The Mind: The Cabinet of Belief Formation.

Think of your mind as the decision-making body where every policy of your life begins. Just like in national governments, the cabinet sets direction, crafts strategy, and determines priorities. In your spiritual government, your thoughts serve the same function: they draft belief systems, write interpretations of your past, and shape your understanding of yourself, others, and God. If your thoughts are laced with fear, rejection, trauma, or unhealed memories, then the "cabinet" is corrupt. A toxic thought life produces chaotic policies rules that say *"Protect yourself at all costs," "Don't trust anyone,"* or *"You'll never be enough."* And these faulty policies eventually leak into every department of your life. That's why Romans 12:2 urges us to be **transformed by the renewing of our mind** because if you want to change how your life is governed, you must begin by rewriting the internal policies of your thought-life.

The Mouth: The Press Secretary of Decree. Your mouth functions like the press secretary communicates what the cabinet has decided. The words you speak, whether privately or publicly, carry legislative weight in the spirit realm. Every statement becomes either an affirmation of truth or an agreement with deception. When you say things like *"I can't," "I'll always be this way,"* or *"That's just how I am,"* you're not just making casual comments you're announcing official decrees that your inner world takes seriously. These statements are not powerless, they **shape your atmosphere**, affect your relationships, and invite spiritual activity (positive or negative) to align with your declarations. Proverbs 18:21 says, *"Death and life are in the power of the tongue."* If your press secretary is continually declaring dysfunction, discouragement, or defeat, then you're publicly endorsing policies that destroy your peace and delay your destiny. When your words begin to reflect God's truth, however, you become the mouthpiece of heaven and your soul government begins to stabilize.

The Movement: The Military that Enforces Policy. Your movement is your body, habits, and lifestyle is the **military** of your internal government. It doesn't draft laws, and it doesn't hold press conferences. It simply does what it's told. In other words, **your behavior follows your beliefs.** When your thoughts are corrupt and your words are negative, your actions can't help but carry out chaos. This is why you might say, *"I want to be healthy,"* but still engage in destructive cycles. The military doesn't make decisions it executes them. That means your habits are **obedient soldiers**, carrying out the orders handed down from the mind and mouth. If your feet keep walking into dysfunction, it's time to review what policies are being written in your thoughts and reinforced by your speech. You can't expect godly behavior while operating under ungodly command. True healing comes when your movement reflects divine leadership, a life where your steps are ordered by the Lord (Psalm 37:23).

When the Soul Government Breaks Down. When your mind is filled with fear, your mouth is soaked in negativity, and your movement reflects trauma or rebellion, your inner government is in disarray. **Proverbs 25:28** captures this vividly: *"He that hath no rule over his own spirit is like a city broken down, and without walls."* Without self-governance, through the help of the Holy Spirit you become vulnerable to every outside influence. Your soul becomes an unguarded city where anything can invade like anxiety, lies, manipulation, or spiritual attack.

God never intended for our soul to be governed by dysfunction.

He designed you to rule with wisdom, righteousness, and peace. That starts by inviting Him to sit on the **throne of your inner government** replacing toxic thoughts with truth, transforming your mouth into a prophetic tool, and realigning your movement to match heaven's mission. Then we can reframe any statement. **Here is an Example of Reframing a Statement**

REFRAMING: Removing Negative Patterns

NEGATIVE PATTERN STATEMENT. That day I typed the phrase "I don't have any...", I instantly heard in my spirit, "DELETE THAT." I knew I had just typed a spiritual agreement with lack.

REWRITTEN AS: "I am in transition, and what I need is

already on its way." Same situation—completely different spirit. Reframing your words doesn't mean ignoring reality. It means choosing the higher truth that aligns with Heaven's perspective.

Who's Ruling in My Soul?

Identifying who is ruling your soul will help you to track your thoughts that have been legislating your life and trace back to the root of those thoughts. You will understand who is really pulling the strings of our soul. The kingdom of light [GOD] or the kingdom of darkness [Satan]. If your soul is a city, it's time to ask: *Who's really on the throne?* Here is the link to the activity for this section below.

JOURNALING ACTIVITY: Who's Ruling in My Soul.

Now that you've taken inventory of your inner government, to reframe your thoughts, your speech, and your movement it's clear that self-governance alone isn't enough. Without the right foundation, even the most disciplined soul will eventually crack under pressure. That's why

God doesn't just want to sit on the throne of your life. He wants to become the foundation beneath it.

True transformation begins when your inner world isn't just managed, but anchored in truth, in grace, and in Him.

The next step in your journey is not simply to change how you govern your thoughts, words, and actions, but to reframe them through God's lens. That means learning how to guard what you think, how to filter what you speak, and how to sanctify what you write not out of fear, but from a place of freedom, identity, and authority. In the next section, we'll explore how to build a Sound Spiritual Foundation that keeps your inner world secure, stable, and aligned with heaven so that what you construct with your life won't just look good... it will last.

1.6 SOUND SPIRITUAL FOUNDATION

The sound spiritual foundation **you build is only as strong as what you build it on.** It doesn't matter how well you manage your thoughts, shape your speech, or discipline your habits if the foundation underneath is cracked, your progress will always be unstable. A sound spiritual foundation is what keeps your inner government grounded in God's truth rather than drifting in self-effort, emotion, or external validation. It begins by allowing God's Word to reframe how you **think**, how you **speak**, and what you **write**. When we filter everything through His wisdom, we're not just maintaining control, we're guarding our soul with spiritual intelligence. Philippians 4:8 tells us to think on what is true, noble, right, pure, lovely, and admirable. This is a divine reframing. It's a command that serves as a mental filter and a spiritual defense system. In this section, we will explore how to build and maintain a secure foundation that safeguards your transformation not just for a moment, but for a lifetime.

The Bible tells us in Romans 12:2, "Be transformed by the renewing of your mind." And James 3 reminds us how powerful the tongue is like a rudder steering the ship of your life. The Word teaches that we are made in the image of God who created with words. If God framed the world by what He said, how much more should we guard what we think, speak, and write? This transformation is done by the renewing of our minds.

Transformation isn't instant, it's architectural. Romans 12:2 doesn't just say *"be changed,"* it says, *"be transformed by the renewing of your mind."* This verse gives us a divine blueprint. If we want to remove toxic patterns and live in sustained freedom, we must submit to a daily process of mind renewal. The word "renew" means to renovate, to restore to a better state. That means tearing down false beliefs, clearing out emotional clutter, and replacing old ways of thinking with truth from God's Word. It's not enough to rebuke a pattern you must replace it with a principle. Renewing your mind is how you lay the spiritual concrete your life can stand on. Without it, your transformation will be temporary. But with it, you create the mental stability needed to uphold long-term change. Long-term change is accomplished when our tongue becomes the rudder that steers our spiritual house.

James 3 tells us that the tongue is like a rudder on a ship small but incredibly powerful. This means your words don't just reflect your thoughts, they determine your direction. Every sentence you speak is like a steering command over your life, nudging you toward victory or vulnerability. Negative speeches, especially about your identity, purpose, or future create cracks in your spiritual foundation. That's why removing negative speech is more than just positive thinking; it's spiritual warfare. Speaking the Word of God over yourself isn't empty affirmation, it's anchoring. It's cementing God's design into your daily walk. If you want to go somewhere different in life, you must let your tongue prophesy your destination, not rehearse your devastation. Understanding that we are made in the image of a SPEAKING God will help us to use our tongue to prophesy to secure our future.

Genesis tells us that we are made in the image of God, and what did God do when He wanted to create? HE **spoke** and said, *"Let there be..."* and reality responded.

This divine pattern didn't stop at creation. As image-bearers, we also create with our words not the universe, but our inner worlds, our expectations, and our atmospheres. That means your speech and writing aren't just expressive, they're constructive. When you repeatedly speak or write something, you're not just stating it, you're framing it. That's why when negative thought patterns are left unchallenged and put into writing or repeated aloud, they become spiritual structures that your life begins to build around. But when we frame our life with faith, identity, and alignment with God's truth, we create a dwelling place for destiny that guard against what we think, speak and ultimately write.

If God framed the world by His words, and you were made to follow His example, then it only makes sense that you must guard what you think, speak, and write. What we think, speak and write are gates that allow negative access or release positive energy that shapes our destiny. These three gates mind, mouth, and message are your building tools. Left unguarded, they become open doors for the enemy to plant confusion, fear, or cycles of defeat. But when they are spiritually guarded filtered through Scripture, saturated in prayer, and aligned with your God-given identity they become the foundation stones for emotional, mental, and spiritual stability. Removing negative patterns is only half the battle; building something stronger in its place is the victory. Your new foundation is laid when every thought is made captive, every word is made holy, and every declaration builds what heaven has designed.

3-Gate Reflection: (Think–Speak–Write)

The **3-Gate Reflection on how we Think–Speak–Write)** is powerful and introspective. It is designed to help us **confront, filter, and align** our inner world with the truth of God's Word as we build a **sound spiritual foundation**. It is a culmination of all the revelations and activities in this chapter that confronts how we can remove negative patterns. Repetition is retention. So, you will see familiar instructions design to strengthen your retention.

The following link to [ACTIVITY 9: 3-Gate Reflection (Think–Speak–Write)](#) is structured in a repetitive way to help you guard your gates that build your life.

Monitoring and managing these three gates are key to transition from disruption to divine re-alignment. Keys that remove negative patterns.

DECLARATION: THINK - Gate Reflection

DECLARATION - THINK: *"I cast down every imagination and thought that rises against the knowledge of God. I think on what is true, noble, right, pure, lovely, admirable, excellent, and praiseworthy. My thoughts are holy ground."*

DECLARATION: SPEAK - Gate Reflection

DECLARATION-SPEAK: *"I silence the voice of fear, lack, and limitation. My mouth speaks life, blessing, healing, and alignment with God's Word. I am a prophetic vessel, and my words build the future God has promised me."*

DECLARATION: WRITE - Gate Reflection

DECLARATION-WRITE: *"I break agreement with every written word that does not align with truth. I reclaimed my scribe's authority. My pen is prophetic. I write the vision, the healing, and the destiny God has spoken over my life."*

Removing negative patterns is an intentional pause to evaluate the patterns running your life, often invisibly. Throughout this chapter, you've learned that your mind is where cycles begin, your mouth is where they're reinforced, and your movement is where they manifest. You've uncovered how toxic thought loops can disguise themselves as normal, how self-sabotaging speech becomes a decree in the spirit, and how behavior is not random, it is often a programmed response to unhealed pain.

You discovered that your inner life is not chaos without cause. It's a government, and you are called to lead it with God as the King. Your mind is the cabinet writing laws, your mouth is the press secretary enforcing policies, and your movement is the military carrying it all out. When these aren't aligned with God's truth, dysfunction reigns. But when your internal leadership structure is surrendered and rebuilt on a sound spiritual foundation, you don't just survive life you begin to govern it with grace, authority, and divine clarity.

You've also learned the power of reframing how guarding your thoughts, speech, and written words is not restrictive, but restorative. You've begun the courageous work of identifying negative patterns, tearing down false narratives, and rebuilding a soul that reflects heaven's blueprint.

But now it's time to go deeper.

Deleting is necessary. Disruption is powerful. But some things can't be erased; they must be excavated. There are roots buried in your past wounds, generational patterns, belief systems, and unspoken agreements that continue to reproduce in your present. You don't just need a new routine; you need a spiritual excavation. Excavation that goes beneath the surface and roots out the past.

We're not just editing sentences.

We're editing our souls.

DELETE TH@T

Let's begin the transformation.

Let's dig.

Chapter 2 – ROOT OUT THE PAST

As we transition from Deleting to transformational Digging, we'll discover how the past, especially the parts we've buried shapes our thoughts, our cycles, and even our sense of identity. You'll learn how to trace emotional residue, confront generational strongholds, and heal from events you thought you'd moved on from but never truly resolved. This isn't just about healing your past it's about freeing your future.

Get your spiritual shovel handled by the Holy Spirit. It's time to dig deeper and uproot what's been silently running your life for far too long. For no one knows us best like the Holy Spirit. This isn't about digging to shame yourself or to rehash old pain for the sake of reliving it. This is about digging to uproot, to expose what's been buried beneath years of silence, survival, and surface-level healing. You can't heal what you won't confront, and you can't confront what you refuse to unearth.

There are patterns still running in your life not because you choose them, but because

they were planted without your permission

and never pulled out with intention.

Some came through trauma. Others were passed down generationally. Still others are emotional weeds growing from words you believed about yourself that were never true. These patterns don't just exist in your mind, they're embedded in your reactions, your triggers, your fears, and even your "normal."

But here's the good news, you don't dig alone. The Holy Spirit isn't just your Comforter, He's your Excavator. He knows where the roots are buried because He was there when they were planted. He saw what you forgot, what you suppressed, and what you misnamed as "just the way I am." No therapist, mentor, or friend knows you the way the Holy Spirit does. He searches for the deep things of your spirit (1 Corinthians 2:10), and He is gentle enough to guide your healing without condemnation, but powerful enough to lead you into freedom with authority.

Let the Holy Spirit show you where your tears started. Let the Holy Spirit Walk you back to the moment your trust broke, when shame took root, or when a lie became your identity. With Him as your guide, this isn't just emotional digging, it's spiritual deliverance. So, take hold of the shovel. Hand it to the Spirit. **It's time to dig up what's been digging into you.**

By now, if you've seriously committed to what you

learned in Chapter 1, you will notice the change in your thoughts, editing in your speech, and the shifting in your actions. You've learned to say, "DELETE TH@T" way before negative patterns try to take hold. But what if I told you that deletion alone isn't enough? Just like weeds in a garden, you can cut them down, but unless you get to the root they'll grow back. Because what you don't uproot will keep replanting itself.

2.1 Trace the Source

Tracing the source means that we must expose the ROOT cause. Every belief system has a beginning. Trauma. Abandonment. Rejection. Disappointment. You see, Trauma doesn't ask for permission—it just builds without blueprint, Abandonment is a whispering lie, 'Every rejection is God's Redirection', expectation is the root of disappointment.

Rejection hurts in the moment, but rejection often reveals where you were never meant to remain. When not healed, rejection plants root of insecurity, comparison, and unworthiness. Expectations build silent hopes without honest communication or God-centered alignment, then disappointment sets in. Unhealed, it becomes a root of bitterness and distrust even toward God. Abandonment whispers, 'You're always alone,' even when you're surrounded."

It's not just about who left it's about the *identity* that formed in their absence. Unhealed abandonment makes you fear connection, expect loss, and cling to what breaks you. And when trauma isn't healed, it builds internal structures of survival rather than surrender. It teaches your nervous system to expect danger and robs you of peace in safe places. To refuse, reject and reverse the attack on our peace, we must trace the source and root it out. This is done by digging deeper into the recesses of our soul's memory that abandonment, trauma, rejection and disappointment carved out an unsafe, experiential reality.

Tracing the emotional and spiritual root systems of abandonment, trauma, rejection, and disappointment is a critical part of the healing journey and is necessary to trace the source and *Root Out the Past*. As we dig in deeper, we see that abandonment lies whispers "You're always alone," even when you're surrounded. If not with people or animals or nature, at least with Angelic Host and God himself. For God said that **HE will NEVER LEAVE us or FORSAKE US.** But when we are drowning in abandonment it always looks like someone walking out, emotional absence, inconsistent care, or never being chosen. Whether it was a parent, partner, friend, or leader, being abandoned leaves a wound that whispers, *"You're not worth staying for."* That message often becomes a root that follows you silently into adulthood. You may fear intimacy, overextend yourself to keep people close, or avoid relationships altogether because you've come to expect that everyone eventually leaves. What makes abandonment particularly deceptive is that the root can still affect you even when you're surrounded by love. The presence of people doesn't always silence the fear of being left. The Holy Spirit wants to help you trace that lie back to its source. Was it the parent who was physically present but emotionally absent? Was it the relationship where you gave everything and were still discarded? By identifying the original abandonment wound, you open the door for God to uproot the belief that you are alone and replace it with the truth that He has *never* left you (Hebrews 13:5). We then move on to examine trauma's effect on our peace and safety.

Recall that trauma doesn't ask for permission it just builds without blueprint. Trauma, by definition, is a deeply distressing or disturbing experience but its most dangerous aspect is what it builds afterward. When unhealed, trauma constructs coping mechanisms, personality traits, emotional filters, and even physical responses, all without your conscious permission. Suddenly, your life becomes a house built with bricks of survival instead of a blueprint of purpose. You might respond with fight, flight, freeze, or fawn without even realizing you're reacting to something *that's no longer happening.* That's the sign of an unhealed root. Your present is still shaped by your past. The Holy Spirit, the ultimate Counselor, is ready to walk you through the rubble not to relieve your trauma, but to release it. Ask yourself, where did the fear start? What moment shifted how I trust, love, speak, or expect? Healing begins not with erasing the memory, but with giving God permission to rebuild your internal world based on truth not trauma. Rejection is 'kin' to trauma and reshape your internal view of you if not rooted out. The statement for rejection is "Rejection is God's Redirection." What does this really mean?

Rejection is often painful, but in the Kingdom, it can be prophetic. What feels like loss is sometimes divine preservation. That person didn't choose you, that opportunity didn't open, that platform didn't last not because you weren't good enough, but because God had something better planned. Yet when rejection goes unhealed, it roots itself in your identity. You stop seeing it as protection and start believing you're unwanted. You may become hypervigilant for signs that people don't accept you, or you might sabotage relationships before they can reject you. To uproot this pattern, ask the Holy Spirit to take you back to the first place you felt unwanted. Was it a parent's favoritism? A teacher's comparison? A spiritual leader's dismissal? Once you name the pain, you can replace it with God's truth: "I am accepted in the Beloved" (Ephesians 1:6). The redirection only works if you stop holding onto what He already moved you from. Now let's deal with the emotional pain that disappointment indwells into our soul.

Expectation is the root of Disappointment.

Disappointment occurs when reality doesn't meet your internal script. We all carry silent hopes. They'll love me like I need... That job will fulfill me... This season will finally change everything. But when outcomes don't match expectations, disappointment sets in not just as a feeling, but as a seed that roots in resentment, cynicism, or apathy. If you've experienced frequent or significant disappointment, you may unknowingly begin to protect yourself from hope altogether. This is how unhealed disappointment leads to stagnation, you stop dreaming, stop praying big, stop expecting good. To uproot this, start with this question: Where did I place my expectations on people, timelines, or God Himself? Trace the pain back to the expectation that broke your heart and invite God to reframe it. He is not afraid of your disappointment. In fact, He wants to meet you there and rebuild your hope not in outcomes, but in Him alone, the One who never changes. The root of abandonment, disappointment, trauma and rejection are the result of a watered life that keep producing poison fruits of the soul.

REAL-LIFE EXAMPLES & RELATED RESEARCH

Real-life stories make these abandonments, trauma, rejection, and disappointment tangible and relatable and are designed to help you identify how unhealed roots might be affecting them in subtle but powerful ways.

Example 1: Abandonment

"I still overperform so people won't leave."

Emotional abandonment is a key component of Adverse Childhood Experiences (ACEs), which have been linked to long-term mental health struggles, difficulty forming secure relationships, and overcompensating behavior in adulthood. "An estimated 61% of adults report having experienced at least one form of parental separation, emotional neglect, or household dysfunction during childhood." (CDC-Kaiser ACE Study, 1998–2014)

Sister Validate-Me grew up with a father who was physically in the home but emotionally unavailable. He rarely engaged with her, missed important events, and never affirmed her worth. Though her mother was nurturing, **Sister Validate-Me** always felt she had to "earn" attention. Jude & Shaver (2016) research shows that Children who experience parental absence emotionally or physically often internalize feelings of worthlessness and develop an anxious attachment style, leading to overcompensation and people-pleasing behaviors in adulthood. This was certainly prevalent in **Sister Validate-Me's** life.

As an adult, she constantly over-commits saying yes to things she has no energy for and working twice as hard in relationships to prove her value. When a friend takes too long to text back or a partner seems distant, her heart spirals into panic. She's surrounded by love but still feels like she's always one mistake away from being left. Only when **Sister Validate-Me** began to trace this pattern to her father's emotional absence did she realize she wasn't just busy **she was functioning from the root of abandonment.** Her healing started when she stopped performing for approval and began to rest in the truth that God's love doesn't require striving. If you are like **Sister Validate-Me,** you too can be free today. Just take the time to do the work and root out these painful emotions out of your heart and hand them back to the enemy of your soul, the devil.

Example 2: Trauma

"I shut down when I feel unsafe—even when

nothing's wrong."

Brother Avoidance was 9 years old when he witnessed domestic violence between his parents. Though his father eventually left, the emotional and psychological damage remained. This type of trauma can cause long-term changes in brain structure and function, particularly in the amygdala and prefrontal cortex. These changes can result in persistent emotional dysregulation, hypervigilance, and freezing responses, even when a person is no longer in danger (Van der Kolk, 2014). These changes can cause anyone to move from confidence to avoidance.

Brother Avoidance didn't act out internalizing everything. As a teen and adult, whenever conflict arose even minor disagreements his body would become tense, his heart would race, and he'd mentally detach from the moment. Relationships were hard because he couldn't explain why he "froze up" during arguments or why he avoided emotional intimacy. In many cases traumatic events can cause people to develop Post Traumatic Stress Disorder (PTSD).

"Approximately **70% of adults** in the U.S. have experienced at least one traumatic event in their lifetime, and **20%** go on to develop PTSD." *(National Council for Behavioral Health, 2020).* Many who don't develop full PTSD still experience trauma-related responses like chronic fear, hypervigilance, and emotional detachment often manifesting as unexplained emotional reactions and relational challenges.

It wasn't until counseling and prayer revealed the traumatic memory that **Brother Avoidance** realized, **his body was still reacting to a threat that no longer existed.** The trauma had built a "default reaction" that was sabotaging his present. His breakthrough came when he invited the Holy Spirit to walk him back to that moment and declared: *"I am not in danger. I am safe. I am seen. I am whole."* For all my **Brother Avoidance** out there, receive your healing today by accepting that you are not alone. There are many more brothers and sisters in this world just like you and they have broken free and is thriving in the same world under the guide and leadership of the Holy Spirit. Come on and join them today.

Example 3: Rejection

Studies show that social rejection activates the same brain regions as physical pain, reinforcing the emotional intensity and long-term effects of repeated rejection—especially in formative years. These experiences can severely affect self-esteem and social functioning (Eisenberger, Lieberman, and Williams.,

2003). This study on the effects of rejection and if refection does hurt clearly show that people who experience rejection, have self-talk of **"I always feel like the extra, never the chosen one."**

In the same study by Eisenberger, et al., Brain imaging studies show that social rejection activates the same brain pathways as physical pain, especially in the anterior cingulate cortex and insula. This means that even minor social exclusions or relational dismissals can leave long-lasting emotional effects, particularly if repeated or experienced early in life (2003).

Sister Insecure experiences the same self-talk. She always felt like the odd one out in her family. Her older sister got straight A's and constant praise. Her younger brother was the baby and the family's joy. **Sister Insecure** was the middle child who often got overlooked. At school, she wasn't chosen for teams. In college, her friends formed tighter bonds without her. As an adult, she now struggles with deep-rooted insecurity and self-worth. She often pulls away first in friendships to avoid being "left out," and she silently believes she's not someone people choose just someone they tolerate. When God started healing her heart, He showed her that the rejection she experienced didn't define her identity it defined a *season*, not her *value*. Once she recognized that what she interpreted as rejection was often miscommunication or misalignment, **she was able to rewrite her internal script**: *"I am chosen. I am accepted. I am loved."*

Example 4: Disappointment

"I stopped expecting good things because nothing ever works out."

Unrealistic expectations cause undue and unnecessary stress. And if left unchecked or unresolved it can cause serious, long-lasting emotional and spiritual damage. Unresolved disappointment can also lead to emotional disengagement, fear of hope, and reduced motivation making it one of the most under-recognized roots of emotional stagnation. A study from the American Psychological Association found that **72% of adults** report experiencing major disappointment from unmet expectations in work, relationships, or personal goals—many of which led to long-term discouragement or depressive symptoms. *(APA Stress in America Survey, 2020).*

This is what **Brother Fear-of-Failure** dwelt with. He had big dreams. He prayed, planned, and prepared to launch a nonprofit after college, but after multiple failed attempts lack funding, bad partnerships, and burnout he began to lose faith, not just in the dream, but in God. Over the years, it felt like every time he got his hopes up, something fell apart. Eventually, **Brother Fear-of-Failure** stopped dreaming altogether. He settled into a job that felt safe but unfulfilling. He stopped praying for big things. He stopped hoping. He wasn't angry just numb. During a men's retreat, **Brother Fear-of-Failure** realized his problem wasn't laziness or fear. It was **unhealed disappointment**. A voice of truth took over the communication and the Holy Spirit whispered, *"You've been grieving closed doors I never called you to walk through."* That moment shifted everything. According to Carver, and Scheier, in their 1998 published work related to 'Self-Regulations of Behavior' disappointment stems from unmet expectations and is deeply tied to our cognitive appraisals of those experiences. Chronic disappointment can result in decreased motivation, reduced optimism, and increased emotional suppression or avoidance behaviors. **Brother Fear-of-Failure** clearly exhibited these symptoms of disappointment that is rooted in failed expectations.

However, **Brother Fear-of-Failure** began journaling through his disappointments, surrendered the outcomes, and slowly rebuild his faith not on success, but on trust. And that trust created space for vision again. If you have spent this long reading this book and identify with or know a **Brother Fear-of-Failure** rest assured that today is the day of victory. Accepts the 'still small voice' of the Holy Spirit that is whispering to you right now. Letting you know that you are carefully and wonderfully made. Made in the image of God and your life cannot be wasted. Like Abraham and Sarah, like Elizabeth and Zachariah, Like Joseph and Jesus, you were created for a specific purpose and

PURPOSE CANNOT DIE.

Somewhere along the way, a seed was planted. That seed became a thought, then a belief, then a behavior. Many of us are carrying patterns that didn't originate with us, they were passed down like heirlooms we never asked for. Inherited beliefs like "love must be earned" or "money only comes through struggle" operate in our subconscious like default settings. If you never expose the root, you'll keep reacting to symptoms and calling it fate.

Residue: Generational & Emotional Cycles

Your patterns may be personal, but they are also generational. What your parents, grandparents, or community normalized could function in your life without question. Are you the first one in your family to try and break the cycle? Congratulations, you're a pattern disruptor. But disrupting isn't easy. That residue clings to your emotions, your language, and your default responses. Emotional residue is like spiritual dust if you don't regularly cleanse it, it settles and becomes part of the furniture of your soul.

The Danger of Buried Pain

Let me be clear, silence isn't healing. Just because you've learned to "get over it" doesn't mean it's gone. Buried pain becomes the compost for toxic roots to grow deeper. It affects how you love, how you trust, how you speak, and how you write. Until you name it, you can't change it. Pain doesn't just disappear, it either gets expressed or it gets encrypted into your daily decisions.

Writing is the fruit of a root.

As we said before, nothing just happens. Every behavior, thought, or written word is fruit from a root. If you want to change the fruit, trace the stem, examine the branch, and pull the root. Writing is the visible fruit of invisible roots. When you find yourself repeatedly writing out pain, lack, fear, or failure it's a signal. There is something deeper beneath the surface. And here's the beauty of this truth: the act of erasing written negativity doesn't just affect the present it exposes and disrupts the root system that fed it.

2.2 Uncovering Emotional Roots

Uncovering emotional roots requires more than just identifying surface-level pain involves tracing every reaction, mindset, and behavior back to its spiritual origin. Much like a tree cannot bear healthy fruit if its roots are diseased, our lives cannot produce wholeness if the hidden places of our hearts remain unhealed. The patterns we tolerate, the offenses we carry, **the ways we respond to pressure,** and even the thoughts we accept as truth are often linked to deeply embedded roots. Roots shaped by past experiences, false images, and unexamined beliefs. Power, identity, silence, offense, and emotional reactivity are often the fruit of deeper internal issues. Whether it's the impulse to control, the habit of reacting before praying, or the subtle resentment birthed from a distorted self-image every issue has a root. And the Holy Spirit is the only One who can help us uncover, confront, and uproot what lies beneath the surface. We must remove the rose color lens to help us recognize emotional strongholds, bring them under the light of God's truth, and invite HIM into the deepest places for lasting healing and alignment.

Power Does Not Negotiate

True power, especially that which is rooted in divine authority, does not entertain negotiations with forces that oppose its purpose. When we recognize our identity in Christ and the authority granted to us, we understand that engaging in debates with doubt, fear, or temptation only serves to weaken our stance. Just as Jesus rebuked Satan with the Word, saying, "Away from me, Satan!" (Matthew 4:10), we too must exercise our authority by standing firm on God's truth without compromise. Negotiating with negative influences can lead to confusion and derailment from our divine path.

Don't Negotiate with Terrorists

In the realm of spiritual warfare, the enemy often employs tactics akin to terrorism instilling fear, spreading lies, and causing chaos. Engaging in dialogue or compromise with such forces is futile and dangerous. Ephesians 6:11 advises us to "Put on the full armor of God, so that you can take your stand against the devil's schemes." Our response should be to stand firm, equipped with truth, righteousness, and faith, rather than attempting to reason with destructive forces. By refusing to negotiate, we maintain our spiritual integrity and protect our destiny.

Don't Respond When You Get Upset

Don't immediately react or respond when you get upset. Never react and some things don't need a response. **Learn to know the difference.** Instead, seek the present truth about the matter. You do this by asking the Holy Spirit to show you what God is really saying on the matter. Remember, emotional reactions, especially in moments of upset, can lead to actions that are misaligned with God's will. Proverbs 15:1 remind us, "A soft answer turns away wrath, but a harsh word stirs up anger." Instead of reacting impulsively, we are called to pause and seek the "present truth." That is, we are to inquire of God's current perspective on the situation. This involves prayer, reflection, and consultation with Scripture to discern God's mind on the matter. By doing so, we ensure that our responses are guided by divine wisdom rather than fleeting emotions. The longer we walk with God, we realize that God has a lot to say on EVERY MATTER. The bible even tells us to search the scriptures because out of them we will find eternal life (John 5:39). This means that anything that pertains to our lives we can find in the scriptures or simply just ask the Holy Spirit.

God Requires That We Inquire

A deep relationship with God involves continual self-examination and openness to His guidance. Psalm 139:23-24 says, "Search me, God, and know my heart; test me and know my anxious thoughts." This introspection allows us to uncover hidden motivations, unresolved issues, and areas needing growth. By regularly inquiring about our internal state, we invite God to reveal truths that lead to healing and transformation, aligning our hearts more closely with

HIS. When we inquire of God HIS heart on the matter, God will first show us ourselves. HE will reveal that often, offense is rooted in the image we have of ourselves.

Offense Is Rooted in Our Self Image

Offense often arises when our self-image is challenged or threatened. However, as believers, our identity is not self-constructed but is derived from our Creator. Genesis 1:27 states, "So God created mankind in his own image." Yes, we are made in the image of God. What others say doesn't do much to change our paychecks, family origin and souls. But we spend a lot of time quibbling, arguing, explaining and discussing what others have to say about us. Recognizing that our image is borrowed from God helps us to respond to offenses with grace and understanding. Scholarly research supports this, indicating that feelings of offense are closely tied to one's self-concept and perceived social image. For instance, a study published in *Frontiers in Psychology by Anolli & Ciceri* highlights that offense is often experienced when there's a perceived threat to one's social identity *(2017)*. Meaning that feelings of offense stem from our social standings with our peers, careers, family and other influential associations. What others think about us and how others see us matters more than we want to admit. However, our behaviors and speech also include our silence on things we should speak up about and lack of action says more about what we really believe. We are not only known by the company we keep, but we are also known by our communication and character.

Schwarz (2020) research sheds light on how religious and spiritual individuals or groups process offense. Most of their offense is based on their beliefs and values. So, when they are offended, it takes on a deeper meaning and feelings of the heart. Their visual representations can impact personal identity and the perception of offense. Schwarz goes on to explain how visual and symbolic representations, especially those connected to identity and belief can provoke deep emotional responses, particularly in religious or spiritual individuals. I believe this is because offense for such individuals is not merely about an action or word, it's an **existential blow to the foundation of their value system**.

For many religious and spiritual individuals, their sense of self is inextricably tied to moral frameworks, doctrinal loyalties, and denominational norms. So, when something challenges or confronts those views, it feels less like disagreement and more like **personal dismantling**. Their internal response often becomes, *"If what I believe is questioned, then who I am must be* *questioned too."* This reveals a deeper root issue **image attachment**. Much of their self-worth has been wrapped up in a borrowed image. How they were taught to see themselves through man-made doctrine, religious performance, or cultural expectation not through God's unfiltered lens.

But when you learn to **process offense from God's perspective**, everything shifts. Offense is no longer a reason to defend yourself, but an invitation to **reflect and refine**.

OFFENSE: Invitation to REFLECT and REFINE

God never asked us to protect our image, HE called us to be conformed into **HIS**. When we begin to think with the mind of Christ (1 Corinthians 2:16), we stop needing to be right, respected, or revered and instead long to be realigned. Offense becomes a mirror, not a battlefield. And freedom begins when we can say, *"Lord, how do You see this?"* Instead of clinging to narrow, man-made ideologies that fracture our soul, we adopt God's eternal perspective, which draws us deeper into truth and intimacy with Him. In His presence, we no longer see ourselves through the lens of denomination, pride, or people-pleasing, we see ourselves in HIS image and no longer feel the need to defend what was never ours to protect. That's when true healing begins when we stop guarding borrowed identities and start embracing our God-breathed identity rooted in grace, strengthened in love, and secure in truth. The less we think of ourselves, the less we have to say to God and respond to others that berates our image.

The Closer to God, the fewer the Words

As we draw nearer to God's presence, we become increasingly aware of His majesty and our own limitations. This realization often leads to a posture of humility and silence. Ecclesiastes 5:2 advises, "Do not be quick with your mouth... God is in heaven and you are on earth, so let your words be few." Peter's experience during the Transfiguration illustrates this point. Overwhelmed by the divine encounter, he hastily suggested building shelters for Jesus, Moses, and Elijah, not fully grasping the significance of the moment (Matthew 17:4). This incident teaches us that in the presence of the divine, it's often wiser to listen and absorb rather than speak impulsively. Embracing silence allows us to fully experience God's revelations and respond appropriately.

Now that we've made the case for rooting out the past, here are a few tools that can help uncover emotional roots. These tools don't just help you dig they help you heal.

1. **Journaling**: Let your writing become a mirror. Ask yourself: "Where did this belief come from?" "Who taught me this was true?"
2. **Therapy**: A skilled counselor can help you excavate hidden memories and make connections you can't see on your own.
3. **Prayer Altars**: A sacred space where you lay your heart before God. Bring your history into the presence of the Holy Spirit and ask Him to reveal hidden agreements.

Tracing The Roots

In this section, we dug beneath the surface of behavior, language, and emotional reactions to uncover the hidden roots that quietly shape how we respond to life. From the idea that power does not negotiate to the truth that offense is rooted in a borrowed image, we've seen how spiritual authority, emotional regulation, and identity all are deeply connected to what we've accepted, absorbed, or inherited often without even realizing it. We examined how reaction without reflection leads us into cycles of self-sabotage, and how seeking present truth the mind of God on a matter positions us to respond from revelation rather than emotional reflex.

Here is the link to the EXERCISE that helps you to trace the roots to discover and uncover negative, emotional patterns. ACTIVITY 11: TRACE THE ROOT

Remember that our walk with God requires inquiry, not assumption. God invites us to examine our internal state with HIM, because only the Holy Spirit can show us the truth about ourselves. We cannot afford to hold on to wounded logic or spiritualized trauma and expect to walk in clarity. Furthermore, the insight that offense is often connected to false identity constructs propped up by visual or emotional distortions reminds us that many of our emotional triggers are not from truth, but from illusions. And lastly, the more we draw near to God, the less we speak and the more we listen, recognizing that humility is the gateway to revelation, and silence in His presence often reveals what speaking cannot.

Together, these truths form a compelling case for rooting out the past. Until we expose and uproot the inner systems that are misaligned with God's truth, we will keep producing fruit from contaminated soil. But when we courageously confront what's beneath our responses, invite the Holy Spirit to shine His light on our emotional roots, and yield our inner narratives to God's truth, we break generational cycles and begin to walk in true freedom. This is not just about healing it's about reclaiming your soul's foundation so you can move forward whole, aligned, and unshakeable in your identity and purpose.

Prayer: Search My Roots

Father God,

I come before You with a humble heart, ready to let You search the deepest places within me. I acknowledge that not everything I feel, say, or do is simply a surface issue—some things have been growing underground for years. I've tried to manage the fruit without dealing with the root, but I'm ready to surrender the soil of my soul to You.

Holy Spirit, I invite You in. Shine Your light into the hidden places. Reveal the beliefs, wounds, words, or images that have been shaping my emotions and decisions. Uproot every lie I've accepted, every false identity I've worn, and every toxic seed that was planted by trauma, disappointment, fear, or shame. I give You permission to go back as far as necessary—even into generational places I don't remember—and break every hidden agreement I've made with darkness.

Let truth flood those spaces. Let healing begin where deception once lived. Teach me how to plant new seeds, speak new words, and walk in new patterns rooted in Your Word and presence. I choose to be whole, not just healed. I choose to be rooted in truth. In Jesus' name, Amen.

2.3 Detoxing: Soul from Memory Triggers

Sometimes it's not just the root that keeps us bound, it's the reminders. Triggers embedded in old photos, places, music, or even social media timelines can pull you back into pain like it happened yesterday. Soul detox requires intentional separation. This might mean unfollowing, deleting, or even moving on from certain environments. Your healing must be more important than your comfort. Detoxing the soul from 'Memory Triggers' will help you to understand how to recognize emotional traps, navigate through them, and prioritize their healing with intentional action.

Healing from your past isn't just about uprooting the source of your pain, it's about recognizing and removing the emotional landmines that keep you cycling through it. You can pray, fast, and journal through a wound, but if your environment is soaked in subtle reminders, it becomes difficult to live in sustained freedom. This is where soul detox comes in because emotional triggers are echoes of the past.

Triggers aren't always traumatic explosions. Sometimes, they're quiet cues a song, a scent, a street name, a photo, or a memory embedded in your social media feed that reopen wounds you thought were closed. Triggers live in the subconscious. You may not even realize you're responding to one until your emotions shift, your heart races, or you suddenly feel sad, angry, rejected, or unsafe without knowing why. This is not weakness it's a sign that your soul remembers. Healing means not just digging up the root, but learning to clear the soil around it, so nothing toxic continues to grow. So, intentional separation is spiritual strength.

Soul detox often requires a level of intentional separation that feels extreme but it's necessary. That might look like:

- Unfollowing or muting social media accounts that keep you emotionally bound to someone or something
- Deleting old texts, voicemails, or photos that serve as anchors to seasons you've already left
- Avoiding certain places or people (at least temporarily) that continually pull you into emotional relapses
- Replacing old playlists, journal entries, or rituals with new, healing habits

This isn't about pretending something never happened, it's about protecting your progress. It's not bitterness. It's boundary. When your peace becomes sacred, you realize that your healing must be more important than your history and certainly more important than your comfort. Comfort will keep you scrolling timelines of the past. Healing invites you to build what's ahead and deny the pain of the past to have power in your present or future.

If something can still emotionally disarm you with a

memory, it still has too much power. And what still has power must be brought under spiritual submission. That doesn't mean you're failing. It means there's more to detox and that's okay. Soul detox isn't a one-time purge. It's a spiritual discipline that must be revisited as you heal in layers. The goal is not to erase your past, but to strip it of its authority over your peace. When you're no longer emotionally hijacked by old triggers, you're not just free, you're whole. So, to be truly free, you must ask yourself the following:

- What needs to go?
- What "harmless" items or media still trigger unhealed emotion in me?
- Am I holding onto anything that serves my nostalgia but sabotages my progress?
- Where have I confused familiarity with freedom?

Do this short spiritual excavation as a quick in 'the-moment' action while your mind is thinking on this subject. Begin by writing a short list titled **"It's Time to Let Go Of…"** and include people, platforms, pictures, or places that need to be lovingly released so that your soul can breathe again.

Spiritual Excavation – PRAYER GUIDE

Your spiritual excavation begins by writing

down the following:
- What's a negative belief I keep repeating?
- What emotion is usually tied to that belief?
- When did I first feel or believe this?
- Who or what planted this seed?
- What truth can I plant in its place?

Then Pray the Following:

"Holy Spirit, reveal the roots I've ignored. Shine a light on the agreements I've made knowingly or unknowingly. I give You permission to excavate what has been buried, so I can walk in healing, not hiding. In Jesus' name, Amen."

Spiritual Excavation Mindset

A spiritual excavation mindset is designed to help you dig deeper into your inner world, uncovering the beliefs, emotions, and experiences that have taken root and shaped how you think, speak, and behave. Find a quiet space, take your time, and invite the Holy Spirit to reveal what needs to be uprooted and healed.

In addition to the quick spiritual excavation action and the prayer guide, here is the link to the [ACTIVITY 10: Spiritual Excavation Worksheet](#)

It's time to stop living from a past you didn't choose.

The soil of your soul is about to be renewed. Let's start digging deep because what's planted next will bear the kind of fruit that rewrites generations. Let's learn how to walk into the now and discover how to Rewrite the Present with power, clarity, and intention.

2.3.1 Healing Soul Wounds

One of the most overlooked realities of soul wounds is this, sometimes, part of you never left the place where the pain happened. You grew up. You moved on. You got the job, the house, the degree. But your soul didn't come with you—at least not all of it.

Soul Segmentation causes emotional detachment from internal soul wounds fragment and requires healing to restore the soul through intentional surrender and spiritual repair. Segmentation happens when your soul left in that moment that you couldn't handle the trauma. The moment of trauma whether it was abandonment, betrayal, assault, neglect, or grief was too much to process, so your soul "segmented" to survive. That part of you froze in time, emotionally and spiritually stuck at the scene of the injury. It may show up as a younger version of you that still panics, lashes out, avoids conflict, or shuts down without explanation. In addition, our memories are also fragmented when the soul fragments due to trauma or overwhelming emotional experiences, the memory system can also fragment.

When a traumatic or overwhelming event occurs, especially one that involves fear, betrayal, abandonment, or abuse the brain and the soul react simultaneously. The amygdala (the brain's fear center) becomes highly active, while the hippocampus (which processes and organizes memory in narrative form) can become inhibited or even shut down. As a result, the brain often stores traumatic memories in disconnected, fragmented ways.

This means you may remember parts of an experience like a smell, a flash of emotion, a voice, or a specific image but not the full story. That's fragmentation. The emotional intensity becomes embedded in the body or soul without the clarity of conscious understanding. This is why a person might be triggered without knowing why. The triggers manifest as you feeling anxious in certain places or situations, they "don't remember." Emotionally shut down or "go blank" during similar experiences later in life.

This correlates deeply with the spiritual reality of soul fragmentation, where parts of the self are emotionally stuck in places the memory hasn't yet named or integrated. This is well-documented in neuroscience, psychology, and trauma research, particularly in the study of dissociation, trauma related memory, and emotional memory processing. Van der Kolk explains that the 'Body Keeps the Record & Score' of every traumatic experience (2014). Many traumatic experiences are often not integrated into normal memory systems, which is why they remain disorganized and fragmented both emotionally and neurologically. This points to memory fragmentation as a clinical symptom of trauma and emotional overwhelm, where memory is stored in dissociative compartments rather than cohesive narrative form.

What science describes as neurological dissociation, the Bible often describes as the soul being "broken," "scattered," or "wounded" (Psalm 147:3). In both cases, parts of our emotional and cognitive self are no longer synchronized. That's why healing the soul also requires the Holy Spirit's guidance in healing the memory both what we recall and what we don't. So, we need our soul to be restored. Restore means "to bring back," "to repair," "to gather again." This includes both the soul and the lost, broken memories within it. This is not the same as ordinary forgetfulness. There is a distinct difference between ordinary forgetting and the inability to recall important autobiographical information especially in the context of trauma or soul wounds.

The normal, healthy process forgetfulness is how the brain manages and stores memory over time. It includes, but is not limited to, forgetting where you put your keys, Not recalling what you ate last Tuesday and Drawing a blank on a childhood friend's name. It is usually caused by distraction or divided attention, passage of time, lack of emotional significance or natural brain aging or memory overload. In these cases, the brain simply doesn't retain or prioritize the memory because it's not essential for survival or identity.

On the other hand, the inability to recall important autobiographical information differs. This is not normal forgetting it's a disruption in the memory system, often linked to trauma or emotional overload.

This can include, but not limited to:

- Gaps in memory about painful or significant life events (e.g., abuse, death of a loved one, assault, abandonment)

- Remembering certain moments *emotionally* (panic, fear, shame) without remembering what happened

- Feeling like something happened, but not being able to put it into words or sequence

This is dissociative amnesia or memory fragmentation, where the brain separates the event from conscious recall to protect you from emotional overload. It's a self-defense mechanism not a failure of intellect. These "missing" memories are often stored nonverbally or somatically in the body, emotions, or subconscious and may resurface in unexpected ways like:

- Triggers without explanation
- Vivid dreams
- Sudden emotional shifts
- "Déjà vu" or reliving the past

Forgetfulness vs. Inability to Recall

Feature	Ordinary Forgetting	Trauma-Linked Memory Gaps
Cause	Time, distraction, low importance	Trauma, emotional overload, dissociation
Type of Information	Trivial or mundane details	Personally significant, emotionally heavy
Recall	Can often be	Often blocked or

Feature	Ordinary Forgetting	Trauma-Linked Memory Gaps
Potential	recalled later	requires healing to access
Emotional Impact	Neutral	Often intense, confusing, or distressing
Storage Location	Easily accessible	Buried in subconscious, body, or fragmented
Healing Path	Not needed	Requires emotional or spiritual restoration

This kind of memory loss is why inner healing and soul restoration is so important. Just because you don't remember what happened doesn't mean it's not affecting you. The Holy Spirit is the only one who can bring to light what was buried, not to shame you but to heal you. The bible says that "The spirit of man is the lamp of the Lord, searching all the innermost parts of his being."(Proverbs 20:27). We need the help of the Holy Spirit as a search light within our soul to help us root out the source of trauma disturbing our souls.

This is why some people feel **deeply disconnected** in their present life. Everything seems "fine," but inside, there's a gap a distance they can't explain. They may say:

- *"I don't feel fully present in my own life."*
- *"It's like part of me is still grieving something I can't name."*
- *"I don't know why I feel stuck here when nothing's actually wrong."*

This isn't dramatic. It's evidence that part of their soul is still stuck in an unfinished moment. You just don't know how to begin healing.

Most people don't recognize that they're fragmented because they were never taught that emotional trauma causes spiritual disconnection. They weren't given language for "soul loss." So even when they do become aware that something is missing, they don't know how to find it or what "collecting the soul" even means. Some try to "move on" by ignoring the pain. Others try to perform their way out of it. But what's needed is spiritual re-collection, an intentional invitation for the Holy Spirit to lead them back to the place of the wound so healing can be completed and wholeness restored. Only the Holy Spirit knows where you lost yourself and the only one that leads you to reclaim your soul.

You can't 'WILL' your way back to wholeness. Only the Holy Spirit knows where you lost that piece of yourself and only the Holy Spirit knows how to gently retrieve it. Scripture says in *Psalm 23:3*, "He restores my soul." The Hebrew word for "restore" literally means to bring back, to return to repair. God specializes in gathering the fragmented, exiled pieces of you that trauma tried to scatter and reintegrating them into wholeness.

You must reclaim your soul.

Prayer to Reclaim Your Soul

Holy Spirit, show me where I left part of myself. Lead me back not to relive the pain, but to recover what was taken, frozen, or shut down. Restore my soul. Bring me into full emotional and spiritual wholeness. I give You permission to walk with me into every memory I buried and bring healing into every space I left behind.

You don't have to figure out the full journey today. All you need to do is BEGIN and the Holy Spirit will lead you the rest of the way.

Again, when we go through intense emotional pain, betrayal, loss, abuse, abandonment, trauma our soul doesn't always process it all at once. Instead of full healing, we often experience what's known spiritually and psychologically as soul wound segmentation. This is the silent fracturing of our inner being where different parts of the soul become frozen in pain, hidden in memory, or emotionally detached from the rest of who we are.

You may feel like you're doing well in one area of life professionally successful, socially connected, spiritually active but completely stuck in another, like emotional intimacy, trust, or self-worth. That's segmentation. It's when your soul heals in patches but leaves certain rooms of your heart boarded up, unvisited, or unaddressed. These "split-off" segments become invisible vaults of unresolved emotion, grief, or fear. And while the rest of you move forward, those parts still relive the memory as if it's happening now. If we don't press and push to move forward then emotional detachment will continue to mask our soul wounds, making you feel like what you are experiencing is normal. But it is just a protective or coping mechanism outside the will of God.

Many people develop emotional detachment as a protective mechanism. When a wound is too painful or repeated too often, the soul learns to compartmentalize it buries the pain in silence to preserve functionality. You may not cry about it. You may not talk about it. But that doesn't mean it's gone.

You've just placed it in an internal holding cell. Emotional detachment can feel like strength on the outside, but inside, it often signals a soul that hasn't been given space to heal. If left unaddressed, soul wound segmentation creates contradiction. You say you're free, but part of you still grieve. You believe in love, but part of you still flinches. You've moved on but not all of you have moved forward. In order for all of you to also move forward, your soul must be healed and restored.

Psalm 23:3 says, "He restores my soul." This isn't poetic fluff it's a divine necessity. Only the Good Shepherd knows how to gather every fragmented part of your soul and make it whole again. Restoration is different from relief. You can feel better and still be broken. Restoration means God reintegrates the fragmented pieces, heals the ruptures, and repairs the inner world that pain tried to destroy.

Here's a practical way to begin reclaiming your soul:

1. Identify the Segmented Places: Ask the Holy Spirit:

- What area of my life feels stuck in the past season?
- Are there parts of me I've silenced, ignored, or numbed just to survive?
- What relationships or experiences made me

emotionally split off from myself?

You may notice a defensive wall in relationships patterns, a part of you that "checks out" during conflict, or a numbness where there should be joy. These are entry points for healing. There's a saying, the biggest room in any house is the room for improvement, so invite God in to renovate your segmented soul.

2. Invite God Into the "Boarded Up" Rooms

Healing doesn't start with fixing it starts with inviting. The parts of your soul that have been silenced by trauma or shut down by pain don't need your perfection they need God's presence. Invite the Holy Spirit into the exact memory, emotion, or place you've avoided. Say something like, "God, I give You permission to enter the places I've blocked off even the ones I've forgotten. Restore what's fragmented. Redeem what's been wounded. Reunite me with myself."

3. Speak Wholeness Over Your Soul

Just like David did in Psalm 42:5 when he said, "Why, my soul, are you downcast? Put your hope in God…" you too must speak life over your own soul. Decree that your soul will no longer live in segments but be restored under the Lordship of Jesus Christ.

Declaration: "My soul will no longer be fragmented by what hurt me. The same God who saved me will restore every part of me. I will feel again, trust again, and walk whole again—mind, will, and emotions aligned with heaven."

4. Journal the Parts of You That Need Healing like:

- "The part of me that still feels _____ needs God's healing."
- "I don't want to stay emotionally numb because _____."
- "I believe God can restore the part of me that was lost when _____."

Naming is powerful.

What you name, you can surrender. What you surrender, God can heal. You were never meant to live in pieces. And no matter how long ago the wound occurred, God specializes in soul recovery. The parts of you that have been detached, numbed, silenced, or forgotten are not lost, they're waiting to be restored. Let God gather the fragments, breathe on them, and make you whole again.

Here is a heartfelt and Spirit-led Prayer for Emotional Detachment from Memory Triggers, to guide you into surrender, healing, and freedom from the emotional pull of the past.

Prayer: Memory Triggers Detachment

"He restores my soul..." – Psalm 23:3. MOST HIGH GOD & Father,

I come to You as the One who knows my past, my present, and my deepest places of pain. You see the triggers that pull me backward even the ones I don't fully understand. You know the songs, images, places, people, and memories that cause my soul to ache and replay old pain like it just happened yesterday. I've tried to move on, but some days I still feel tied to what I thought I'd let go of. So today, I surrender all.

Father, I lay every emotional memory at Your feet. The images, the timelines, the conversations, the disappointments. The part of me that still mourns what was or what should have been. I ask You, Holy Spirit, to sever every soul tie that no longer serves my healing.

Break emotional agreements I've made with people, places, seasons and songs. Untangle me from the attachments that keep me emotionally cycling. Let Your peace uproots what my pain tried to bury.

Give me the courage to unfollow what disturbs my spirit. To delete what no longer belongs in my today. To make space for what You are trying to build in my tomorrow. Let me honor the past without being enslaved to it.

Rewire my nervous system to respond with the truth instead of trauma. Cleanse my memory from being a place of torment and turn it into a testimony.

In Jesus Christ Name Amen.

This prayer, along with the activities and content in this Chapter 2: Root Out the Past have helped you to go beneath the surface. You've allowed the Holy Spirit to hand you a spiritual shovel and walk with you into the unseen places not just to revisit the past, but to uproot what's been silently sabotaging your present.

We explored how **soul wounds, fragmented memories**, and **unhealed trauma** can anchor parts of us in places we thought we had left. You discovered that the past doesn't always speak loudly but it always leaves a residue. And unless you remove the root, the pattern will replant itself.

From abandonment to trauma, rejection to disappointment, we traced how **emotional pain becomes spiritual architecture** building false identities, shaping our expectations, and programming behaviors that contradict our healing. But through intentional surrender, prayer, and soul excavation, you've taken the first steps toward becoming whole again not just in memory, but in movement. You've learned that

Healing is not passive, it's a Partnership.

And now that you've started the work of uprooting what no longer belongs, your soul is ready to build something better. But now comes the invitation to **do something new.** With the space you've cleared it is time to learn how to rewrite the present. You can't move forward by copying and pasting the past. God doesn't just want to heal what happened He wants to help you rewrite how you live now.

Your present no longer must echo old stories. It can become the blank page where truth, identity, and freedom begin to move forward.

Let's step into it on purpose.

Chapter 3 – REWRITE THE PRESENT

Let's be honest many of us are living recycled lives. We're repeating old language, making default decisions, and reacting out of muscle memory instead of divine intention. But here's the truth, you can't rewrite your life if you're still copying and pasting your past. The past may have been painful, but it doesn't have to be permanent. What you decide to write today sets the stage for what shows up tomorrow.

3.1 Power of Present-Tense Authority

One of the greatest shifts you can make is learning to speak and write in the present tense. Not "I will be," but "I am." Not "One day I'll have," but "I have everything I need for today." When you embrace present-tense authority, you're not lying to yourself you're aligning yourself with God's reality. Scripture reminds us in Hebrews 11:1 that faith is now. It doesn't wait for everything to look perfect it speaks what is unseen as if it already exists. You must use faith to rewrite your soul narrative to manifest the present you want. One way is to rewrite self-talk and identity statements.

Rewriting Self-Talk and Identity Statements

Though the concept of self-talk was introduced in Chapter 1, I want to explore Self-talk from the perspective of a person's internal narrator. As a refresher, self-talk. What we speak to ourselves silently is just as influential as what we say over our children or environment out loud.

We all have an internal narrator the voice inside that explains, justifies, critiques, or defines what's happening in our lives. For many, that voice has been shaped by pain, loss, rejection, or comparison. Instead of encouraging us, it accuses. Instead of guiding us, it shames.

Many of us have allowed self-talk, our internal narrator, to become a harsh critic or a passive bystander. It's time to take the pen back. Begin rewriting your internal dialogue with truth. Instead of "I always mess up," say "I am growing wiser with every decision." Instead of "I'm not qualified," declare "I'm equipped by grace and led by purpose." These are not just statements they are bricks in the foundation of a new identity. It is time to take the pen back from our internal self-talk narrator.

But here's the truth, you have the authority to

rewrite your inner dialogue. You are not stuck with the voice of your wounds. You can trade the internal critic for a Spirit-led narrator that speaks from truth and identity, not trauma and insecurity. These rewrites aren't wishful thinking they are declarations of faith, laying the foundation for a new way of living.

Example 1: Rewriting Dating Self-Talk

From "I'm Hard to Love" to "I'm Worth Pursuing in Wholeness"

When dating has been marked by rejection, ghosting, or cycles of unhealthy relationships, it's easy for your internal narrator to conclude, *"I must be the problem."* Many people silently tell themselves, *"I'm too much," "I'm too broken,"* or *"I always mess this up."*

But that kind of self-talk keeps you emotionally tethered to the wounds of your past. It forms your dating identity around failure rather than growth. So, rewrite this self-talk as:

"I am learning. I am healing. I am worth pursuing in wholeness. God is teaching me discernment, not disqualifying me from love."

REAL-LIFE EXAMPLE:

After a string of emotionally unavailable

relationships, **Sister Waiting-On-Love** started believing that she was "too needy" or "too intense." But in therapy and prayer, she realized she had been trying to prove her worth rather than receiving love from a healed place. She rewrote her self-talk and began dating from a place of confidence rather than craving. Her relationships shifted when her self-narrative changed.

Example 2: Miscarriages

From "My Body Failed" to "My Heart is Still Whole"

Loss through miscarriage is devastating—not only physically but emotionally and spiritually. Many women and couples internalize this loss as personal failure, and their self-talk becomes haunted by shame: "My body is broken," "I did something wrong," or "I'll never be a mother."

This grief is real, but the identity built around the pain is not the truth. Rewrite the self-talks as: *"My womb is not a measure of my worth. My loss is not a label. I am whole, even in grief. And God still writes beautiful endings."*

REAL-LIFE EXAMPLE:

Sister FRUITFULL, after two miscarriages,

stopped attending baby showers and avoided pregnancy announcements. Her self-talk was wrapped in bitterness and guilt. But after attending a women's retreat where she received prophetic encouragement and inner healing, she began speaking life over herself again even before conceiving. Her joy returned before her circumstance changed.

Example 3: Divorce

From "I Failed at Marriage" to "I'm Free to Heal and Grow"

Divorce can create an identity crisis. Even if the relationship was toxic or irreparable, the soul often whispers, "I failed," or "I'll never have real love again." This internal script can become a cycle of shame and secrecy, especially in spiritual communities.

But divorce is not your identity, it's an event, not your essence. Rewrite the self-talk as: "That chapter has closed, but I'm still worthy of love, peace, and purpose. I'm not disqualified; I'm being rebuilt."

REAL-LIFE EXAMPLE:

Brother Love-Lost, a former pastor, went through a painful divorce and lost much of his community. His self-talk became toxic: "I'm a disappointment to God." But after months of counseling and re-engaging with God's Word, he began to say: "I'm not defined by what broke me, but by Who is rebuilding me." He later launched a support group for divorced men, helping them rewrite their stories too.

Example 4: Parenting

From "I'm Not Doing Enough" to "I'm Called for This Season"

Parenting brings out every insecurity, especially in single parents or those raising children after trauma. Many parents carry silent guilt: "I'm messing my kids up," "I can't give them enough," or "I don't know what I'm doing." This kind of self-talk breeds anxiety and comparison, rather than peace and presence.

Rewrite the self-talks as: *"God trusted me with this assignment. I don't have to be perfect—I just have to be present. I am the right parent for this child."*

REAL-LIFE EXAMPLE:

MAMA-GRATEFUL, a single mother of three, used to cry herself to sleep feeling like she was failing. One night during prayer, she felt God speak, "They need your love, not your perfection." She started affirming herself daily, saying: "I'm a grace-filled guide, not a flawless machine." Her peace returned and so did her confidence.

At the end of the day, we all need to speak to our soul like the way God speaks to us. We can take a note out of David's book when he said, 'Why are you cast down of my soul...hope though in God' (Psalm 42:5). David modeled this beautifully when he paused in a moment of despair and he didn't ignore his pain, he challenged it. He didn't let his feelings dictate the final word; he gave his soul a new direction.

HOPE THOU IN GOD.

That's what rewriting your self-talk truly is learning to speak to your soul the way God speaks to you. Instead of rehearsing every failure, you remind yourself of God's faithfulness. Instead of echoing anxiety, you declare His promises. Your soul may be tired, discouraged, or confused but your spirit, anchored in truth, can take the lead. When you take back the pen from your pain and let God's Word author your self-talk, your inner world begins to align with your divine identity.

This is how healing gets rooted, and destiny gets unlocked. The most powerful transformation begins not with changing our circumstances, but with changing how we speak to ourselves. Your internal narrator should sound like the Holy Spirit not your history.

Every time you rewrite a lie with truth, you're not just shifting your mindset you're reconstructing your identity on the foundation of God's Word. Your new chapter begins with a new confession.

Living by Your Vision, Not Your History.

Your History May Explain You,

But Don't Let It Define You.

The goal is to live from vision not memory. Ask yourself: What does the future version of me look like? How does she/he speak, walk, work, love, and lead? And what can I start doing today that aligns with that version? Every aligned action is a vote for your healed self. Start casting votes that affirm your growth. Casting votes for your own life is like voting for your own dominance in the narrative you are rewriting. This dominance becomes governance. Governance becomes written policies for your soul. This way you rewrite the policies from the Holy Spirit that will govern your inner man. Your inner man govern by the Holy Spirit is considered by God as a city (Proverbs 25:28).

3.2 Rewriting Policies in Your Inner Man

Here's where it gets deeper. When you write a new policy, that becomes a new language (i.e. self-talk). Basically, you're issuing new government policies for your inner city. Remember Proverbs 25:28: "He that hath no rule over his own spirit is like a city that is broken down, and without walls." You are the lawmaker and the enforcer of your present. Your mind drafts the law. Your mouth decrees it publicly. Your movement enforces it physically. So, ask yourself what laws you have been living under? And are you ready to abolish the old policies and legislate **healing, truth, and wholeness? To correctly answer these questions, we must develop the concept of rewriting policies that govern the inner man with deeper insight,** new language, and powerful spiritual revelation.

You are the lawmaker and the enforcer

Whether you realize it or not, your inner world functions under a **personal constitution**al set of silent laws, emotional contracts, and spiritual decrees that dictate how you think, react, speak, and show up in life. These "policies" aren't just beliefs. They're deeply ingrained systems, usually written in pain, fear, or past experience, and enforced by your daily behavior. But here's the truth, **you wrote those laws, and with God's help you can rewrite them.**

3.1.1 Your Mind Drafts the Law

Every belief you've carried about yourself, others, or God began as a thought. Whether rooted in truth or trauma, your mind acts like a legislative chamber, constantly drafting policies that get internalized as facts: *"People can't be trusted," "I always mess things up," "I don't deserve more,"* or *"Love always ends in pain."* These thought-formed laws may feel like protection, but often, they're bondage disguised as boundaries. Until you confront them, they become the legislation of your life, deciding what you pursue, avoid, or settle for.

Truth to Remember: Just because a thought is familiar doesn't mean it's righteous. And just because it was passed once, doesn't mean it must remain law. And not all thoughts are ours, and we must examine every thought before allowing it to become part of our self-talk or soul governance.

One of the most critical revelations in renewing the mind is this, not every thought that enters your mind originated from you. Your thoughts come from many sources of past experiences, family systems, cultural programming, trauma, spiritual influence (divine or demonic), media consumption, and emotional state. Some thoughts are whispers from heaven. Others are fiery darts from the enemy (Ephesians 6:16). Some are echoes of your upbringing, while others are survival mechanisms developed in painful seasons. Yet because they arrive in *your* head, you assume, they belong to you. NEWS FLASH:

Every thought in your head,

DOESN'T come from you.

And this is where many people fall into agreement with deception. The enemy doesn't need to control your life, he only needs you to adopt a thought and enforce it as law. Once it becomes your inner dialogue, you begin building your identity and actions around it and believe the thoughts in your head that says:

- "I'm too much."
- "I'm too much."
- "I don't belong anywhere."
- " Nobody will ever understand me."
- "I'll never recover from this."
- "I always ruin things."

These aren't just words. They are unvetted thoughts turned into legislation governing how you show up in relationships, prayer, work, love, and even how you perceive God.

Thoughts Must Be Vetted, Not Voted In.

In a natural government, a proposed law must be reviewed, debated, and vetted before it becomes policy. But in the soul, most people skip the review process and adopt thoughts simply because they *feel true*. But not all feelings are faithful, and not all thoughts are trustworthy. That's why Scripture tells us to *"Take every thought captive to make it obedient to Christ."* — 2 Corinthians 10:5.

3.1.2 Capture What Is Trying to Capture You

The word **"take captive"** implies interrogation. This is interesting. I take this meaning as,

I WILL CAPTURE,

WHAT IS TRYING TO CAPTURE ME.

You don't let every thought waltz into your mind and sit at your decision-making table. Don't be lazy. DO THE WORK to regulate your own soul and ask the following until you get an answer. DON"T RUSH THE PROCESS. Wait for God to answer. It may be instant, or it may take a day. It may come when you are in the kitchen chopping onions, then the Holy Spirit will whisper in a still small voice:

- *Where did you come from?*
- *Do you line up with truth?*
- *Are you speaking in alignment with God's Word or my wounds?*
- *If I believe you, what fruit will you produce in my life?*

This spiritual discipline becomes your thought filter ensuring that only thoughts aligned with healing, identity, truth, and divine purpose get written into your inner law book.

Learn To Repeal What You've Previously Passed

The thoughts that became laws in seasons of pain don't have to remain active legislation today. Just because your mind once agreed with,

"I'm always rejected," doesn't mean you have to keep enforcing that law in every new friendship or opportunity. Work on refusing, rejecting and reversing these thoughts that are not of God by:

- **Identify** the origin of the lie
- **Revoke** your agreement with it
- **Replace** it with God's truth

Your soul is not a dictatorship of brokenness. It's a living kingdom where you, submitted to the Spirit of God, have the authority to reform your inner government.

Legislative Thought Tracker

Here is a link to [ACTIVITY 12: Personal Legislation-Thought Tracker]() identify, revoke and replace every evil decree you have spoken. Remember, just because it sounds like you, doesn't mean it belongs to you. Every thought must be tested before it becomes truth in your system. Your mind acts as a legislative floor so use it to guard what becomes law.

3.1.3 Your Mouth Decrees the Law

Once thoughts become law, your mouth gives them public authority. Every time you speak something over yourself whether in frustration, fear, or false humility you are verbalizing a policy that your soul begins to enforce. Saying things like *"I'm just not built for relationships,"* or *"Money never stays with me,"* or *"I can't change"* might feel like venting but in the spirit, it functions as a legislative decree. And what you decree, you authorize. This is why Proverbs 18:21 says, *"Death and life are in the power of the tongue."* Your speech doesn't just express your thoughts, it enforces your internal government. If your mouth is still echoing pain, your life will continue to operate under policies written in your woundedness.

Prophetic Principle:

Words don't just describe reality, they shape it.

3.1.4 Your Movement Enforces the Law

Your behavior is the military arm of your soul government. It carries out whatever policies have been written and decreed internally. If you've believed, *"No one will protect me but me,"* you will live hyper-independent, never asking for help. If you've believed, *"I'm always left behind,"* you will react to people from abandonment even if they haven't left. This is why rewriting your mind, and your mouth must eventually be reflected in your movement. You can't speak healing but walk in the same toxic routines. Your steps must agree with your new laws. And guess what? The moment you take one different step, one movement aligned with healing instead of fear you begin enforcing a **new spiritual regime.**

Identify what laws you have been living under by searching through the residue of thoughts that your trauma left behind. Don't forget to include the seasons of survival, abandonment, or fear that drafted certain narratives and rewrite policies of your soul that were originally written by someone else, you're your parents, culture, religion, or a broken inner voice? If those laws no longer reflect who God says you are, they must be abolished.

It's time to repeal every mental law that contradicts the cross. It's time to revoke every spoken decree that reinforces your dysfunction. And it's time to enact new policies that legislate healing, truth, freedom, identity, and divine purpose. Then write a short "Internal Constitution" that reflects the healed, whole, and Spirit-led version of yourself.

Example Internal Constitution: *"I am governed by grace, not guilt. My thoughts are aligned with truth. My words build life, not limitation. My actions reflect purpose, not pain. I have abolished fear-based policies and installed the law of liberty in Christ Jesus. I am not under the rule of my past I am led by the government of peace."*

Now write your own daily declarations and affirmations that create a rhythm of speaking life over yourself daily. Write a set of declarations that reflect your healed identity and speak to them aloud each morning. Place affirmations in your mirror, in your phone, or wherever you need to see them most. Your words should become a holy echo of Heaven's opinion of you. Ritualize this process. Make it sacred, consistent, and personal.

DECLARATION & PRAYER:

This declaration and prayer spiritually reclaim authority over your mind, discerns the source of your thoughts, and legislates truth over your soul. *"Let the words of my mouth, and the meditations of my heart, be acceptable in Thy sight..."* Psalm 19:14.

I DECLARE: Reclaim Authority

My mind is not a battlefield of confusion, it is a sanctuary of peace. My thoughts are not authored by trauma, they are governed by truth. I am no longer led by default thinking—I am led by divine revelation. I think about what is true, pure, lovely, just, and worthy of praise. My thoughts, my words, and my movement align with the government of Heaven.

I repeal all old laws written in survival mode, and I install truth written by Your Spirit. Every lie is now overturned.

I silence every false narrative. I don't just think differently,

I legislate differently. From this moment forward,

I will not entertain, empower, or enforce thoughts that You didn't send.

I now operate with divine thought authority, under the Lordship of Jesus Christ.

I declare that my mind is renewed, my tongue is disciplined, and my soul is aligned. And it is so, in Jesus' name.

Amen.

Prayer: Enforce Authority

Father God,

I come before You as the rightful steward of my mind no longer a passive recipient of every thought, but an active legislator of truth. I confess that I have, at times, allowed thoughts to live in me that You never sent. I've agreed with lies that were familiar but not faithful. I've enforced inner laws rooted in fear, rejection, shame, and past pain.

But today, I take back my thought life. I renounce every mental law that contradicts the truth of who You've called me to be. I cast down imaginations, assumptions, and unvetted beliefs that exalt themselves against Your knowledge.

Holy Spirit, be the filter of my mind. Teach me to interrogate every thought, examine every motive, and detect every lie before I allow it to write policies over my identity, purpose, or future.

Intentional Self-Healing Language

This self-healing Language is powerful, but transformation requires action. Ask yourself daily: What can I do today that my healed self would do? It might be as simple as organizing your space, speaking up for yourself, investing in your dream, or saying no to something that drains you. The goal isn't perfect, it's congruence. Let your actions match the person you're becoming. Rewrite Your Daily Renewal Narrative by taking 20–30 minutes to complete the following. This is a different approach to an earlier exercise, and it is designed to pull from out of you invisible and hidden works of the enemy that we attribute to normalcy.

Here is the link to [ACTIVITY 13 : Intentional Self-Healing Language.](#)

Discernment Detector

Your present is a powerful place. It is not just a pause between the past and future it's the pen in your hand. Write wisely. Govern boldly. Declare purposefully. Now, let's do another exercise that will help us discern whether our thoughts are from LIES, LAWS or LORD. Here is the link to [ACTIVITY 14: The Discernment Detector](#)

Now that you've done the brave work of silencing the inner critic and handing your internal pen back to truth. In this chapter, you've learned that your self-talk is not just a conversation, it's a construction site.

Every word spoken and every thought entertained has the power to either rebuild your identity or reinforce old patterns. By rewriting your internal policies, replacing toxic talk with transformational truth, and learning to speak to your soul the way God speaks to you, you've begun the process of realigning your life with heaven's narrative. You are no longer living by recycled pain or inherited scripts you are writing the present with purpose, on purpose. You know you have to rewire your future.

So, prepare for the days ahead. Even though it hasn't happened, tomorrow will manifest what was done today. And though those versions of you that haven't been lived yet, your future is not fixed. It's programmable. Just like your past didn't have to be repeated, your future doesn't have to be feared.

Next, we'll discover how your habits, declarations, imagination, and faith write the code for what comes next. Because transformation doesn't just stop with what you believe today it continues in how you build what's ahead. Let's rewire your future line by line, word by word, truth by truth.

It's time to write the right code. As we step into prophetic momentum, we will learn how to Rewire our Future and align our actions with divine destiny.

Chapter 4: REWIRE YOUR FUTURE

What if your future isn't something you simply walk into but something you help write? What if the version of you you're becoming is not hidden in fate, but hidden in your thought patterns, spoken declarations, and repeated behaviors?

Your future isn't fixed, it's flexible. It doesn't just happen to you it's written by you. And just like a computer follows the script of its programmer, your life follows the code you think, speak, and act on. Your future is programmable if you write the right code. Rewiring your future will help you to understand how to architect your tomorrow with purpose, faith, and strategy. That's not just a faith concept, it's science too. Neuroscience that is.

Neuroscience has proven that the brain is capable of neuroplasticity the ability to rewire itself based on what you repeatedly think, say, and do. Every time you reinforce a thought or habit. Your brain forms a neural pathway a mental "trail" that makes it easier to repeat that action again in the future. The more you travel that path, the more automatic it becomes. Whether the thought is truth or trauma, your brain doesn't discriminate, it simply reinforces what you practice. Now pair that with this biblical truth of Romans 12:2 that says, *"Do not be conformed to this world, but be transformed by the renewing of your mind..."*

The Word of God was speaking about **neural renewal** before science ever had a name for it. God knew that if your thoughts didn't change, your life wouldn't either. But He also gave us the process:

Repetition + Revelation = Transformation.

You're not stuck with yesterday's mindset. And that means you're not stuck with yesterday's outcomes because your future can be changed. Your future just doesn't have to be something that happens to you. It can become something that's written by you with every belief you hold, every word you speak, and every action you take. And just like a computer follows the exact instructions of its programmer/coder, your life will follow the internal code you write. So, you rebuild cautiously by re-coding your fears with faith. If your declarations are coded with lack, you will attract limitations, so reprogram them. If your actions are coded with confusion, your direction will stay unstable. But when you rewrite the code with truth, when you install heaven's software your mind, mouth, and movement come into prophetic alignment. That's the spiritual technology of destiny. Rewiring rebuilds with strategy, faith and purpose.

Rewiring your future is more than thinking happy thoughts. It's about becoming the architect of your tomorrow, consciously constructing a life that reflects the blueprint of heaven. It's what happens when faith meets discipline, to break old mental codes that were installed by pain, fear, or generational cycles and script new thoughts that align with God's promises. When prayer meets planning, when obedience meets vision to speak prophetically to your future self and build daily rhythms that support where you're going not just where you've been.

In essence, your tomorrow doesn't need to mirror your past. You're not recycling old blueprints. You're receiving new instructions. It's time to recode, reframe, and rebuild. So, take the time to rewire your future one declaration, one pattern, one renewed thought at a time. You accomplish this with a script that write the life your soul is longing to live or the life that God says is available for you to live.

This is not just a journaling activity it's a prophetic declaration in written form. You're not writing what you *wish* might happen, you're writing what you choose to believe, become, and build. You are giving language to your future, one truth-filled sentence at a time. This is your soul's agreement with heaven.

When you write it,

Your brain begins to create it.

When you read it,

Your spirit begins to align with it.

When you repeat it,

Your life begins to reflect it.

We reflect on life by speaking positively. Positive talks begin with a purposeful narration of how you want to rewire your future. Like a 'Self-Script'

Write A Future Self Script

The Future Self Script is more than a journaling tool—it is a prophetic blueprint and identity rehearsal that trains your mind, mouth, movement, and self-perception to align with

God's truth about your destiny. By writing in the present tense, you activate your brain's neuroplastic capacity to believe, internalize, and live into what you repeatedly declare. Instead of merely hoping for change, you begin inhabiting transformation. This script reshapes your inner language, reorders your decision-making, and helps you respond to life as the healed, whole, and purpose-driven version of yourself. Your mind, mouth, movement, identity, and future reinforces is a multi-dimensional framework that moves you out of survival and into spiritual synchronization with your calling. As you declare your "now" from heaven's perspective, you break agreement with old patterns and build a new internal reality strong enough to carry the future God has already written for you. Here is the link to [ACTIVITY 15: Future Self Script.](#)

    Read the self-script you created out loud every morning for seven (7) days and watch how your mind begins to believe it, your heart starts to feel it, and your habits begin to live it. You will see how scripture and science merge into a undeniable proof that you can indeed rewire your future.

4.1. The Science of Neuroplasticity

Science and Scripture agree on this one truth, change is possible. **Neuroplasticity** is the brain's ability to rewire itself. Your thought patterns, responses, and habits aren't set in stone, they're malleable. And Romans 12:2 confirms it: *"Be transformed by the renewing of your mind."* Every time you choose a new thought, speak a new truth, or act in alignment with God's Word, you're forming new neural pathways and spiritual highways for your destiny. The science of neuroplasticity rewires your brain for destiny.

Neuroplasticity is one of the most powerful, hope-filled concepts in modern science and one of the most spiritually aligned truths in Scripture. It's the brain's built-in ability to rewire and reorganize itself in response to new information, repeated behaviors, learning, or spiritual revelation. You are not locked into old mental patterns. You can change. More than that you were created to change any circumstances.

The Apostle Paul said it like this in Romans 12:2, *"Be transformed by the renewing of your mind..."* That word renewing speaks of a constant, ongoing process not just spiritual cleansing, but mental reprogramming. Let's explore how science confirms the Word and how your brain becomes the soil where your destiny is either starved or seeded. This scripture shows that change is possible because your brain was designed to adapt. So, it doesn't matter when you discover this truth, at that moment, you can decide to change your mind. If you are not lazy and willing to do the work, you'll have the information and tools needed to change your mind.

Neuroplasticity proves that the brain is malleable. Every thought you think, every belief you reinforce, and every habit you repeat sends electrical impulses through neural pathways. When a pathway is used frequently, it becomes stronger easier to access. When it's unused, it weakens and fades. In simple terms:

What you practice becomes permanent.

Even if what you're practicing is

ANXIETY, FEAR, OR SHAME.

But here's the hope, if you created a toxic pathway, **you could also create a healed one.**

Vignette 1: Sister Twisted-Mind Brain Rewiring

Sister Twisted-Mind, a 35-year-old

entrepreneur, had grown up in a home where money was scarce, and struggle was spiritualized. Even after building a six-figure business, her brain still operated from fear of lack. She'd rehearse the same internal script "It'll all fall apart eventually." Through therapy, Scripture-based declarations, and intentional journaling, **Sister Twisted-Mind** began replacing those thoughts with truth: *"I steward increase with wisdom. God's provision is consistent."* After six months, she noticed her spending changed, her giving increased, and her anxiety around money began to dissolve. Why? Her brain had rewired. Her new spiritual identity built a highway of peace where there used to be potholes of fear. Potholes are formed when the road surface cracks, water and traffic. It would be ok if the surface was just cracked by the adding of water into the crack and the constant traffic rolling over those cracks is what makes the potholes worse. For potholes, the small surface cracks form and expand over time with the action of traffic. Water then seeps through the surface of the cracked pavement, causing further deterioration in cold climates, this can be exacerbated by freeze-thaw weathering.

Just like a highway in the natural, your inner life also has roads pathways of thought, memory, emotion, and belief. And where peace should flow freely, many people find themselves stuck swerving around potholes of fear, anxiety, or unhealed wounds. Potholes don't show up overnight. They begin as small cracks in the surface subtle lies, silent disappointments, or ignored pain. Over time, like water seeping in and traffic rolling over those cracks, those small fractures widen and deepen, especially under pressure. In colder seasons of the soul when life hardens or hope feels frozen the damage worsens, and suddenly, what began as a manageable crack becomes a sinkhole in your spiritual and emotional landscape. But here's the truth, the same repetition that formed the pothole can be redirected to rebuild the road. Just as fear was rehearsed into a rut, faith can be repeated on a godly highway. Your spiritual identity isn't meant to live dodging damage, it's meant to construct new roads of peace, purpose, and power. Every repetition becomes a road forming spiritual highway that can carry the weight of your destiny.

Repetition is the key to transformation.

Science shows that the more often you think, speak, or act in a certain way, the more automated that behavior becomes. In the same way you can develop a bad habit through repetition, you can also train your brain to align with spiritual truth. God doesn't just want you to memorize truth He wants you to **wire it** into your being. *"I will put my laws in their minds and write them on their hearts..."* (Hebrews 8:10). That's neuroplasticity and divine impartation working together.

Vignette 2: Forming Spiritual Highways

The Anxious-Man, a youth pastor in his twenties, had always struggled with social anxiety. Speaking in front of others made him nauseous. But he knew his calling required him to teach and lead. That said, he lives a life through the lens of anxiety. That said, he started to do something different. Every morning, **The Anxious-Man** began declaring 2 Timothy 1:7 over himself, *"I have not been given a spirit of fear..."* He rehearsed sermons in front of a mirror. He said affirmations aloud and prayed in the Spirit before meetings. Over time, the fear circuits in his brain weakened, while the confidence circuits strengthened. He didn't just gain courage he built a spiritual highway for his assignment to travel on. This daily dismantling began a new repetitive routine that gradually tears down the old thought life and rebuilds the new. The potholes of the mind were repaired and maintained.

Neuroplasticity also helps to dismantle of old pathways what science calls "synaptic pruning." In neuroscience, synaptic pruning is the brain's natural process of cutting away unused or unnecessary neural connections to make room for more efficient ones. During childhood and adolescence and continuing subtly throughout life the brain evaluates which connections are being consistently used and which are not. Huttenlocher & Dabholkar 1997 study, describes this as Regional Differences in Synaptogenesis in Human Cerebral Cortex.

The concept of regional differences in synaptogenesis in the human cerebral cortex shows how synaptogenesis (the formation of synapses) affects the development of neural pathways especially in connection to how the brain determines which pathways to strengthen and which to prune.

Synaptogenesis is the process by which neurons form synapses, the connections that allow communication between different parts of the brain and nervous system. This process is critical for learning, memory, emotional regulation, and decision-making. But not all regions of the brain develop these connections at the same time or in the same way. In addition, in their landmark 1997 study, Huttenlocher and Dabholkar discovered that different regions of the human cerebral cortex undergo synaptogenesis on different timelines, depending on their function and maturity requirements. For example:

- The visual and sensory cortices, which help process basic information like sight and sound, tend to develop synapses earlier, often peaking in infancy.

- The prefrontal cortex, which governs higher order thinking like decision-making, impulse control, and spiritual discernment, continues developing well into late adolescence and early adulthood.

This means that the timing and density of synaptic formation are region-specific and experience dependent. The more certain pathways are used such as through repeated behaviors, thoughts, or learning the more those synapses are strengthened. Conversely, unused or rarely activated synapses undergo synaptic pruning, a neurological "clean-up" that removes weak or unnecessary connections to enhance mental efficiency.

This process determines which mental "highways" are built. If you repeatedly respond to stress with fear, those neural pathways are strengthened. If instead, you begin to respond with prayer, truth, or spiritual discipline, your brain begins to favor those pathways instead. Over time, synaptogenesis and pruning work together to build or break down the roads your brain travels most often which shapes everything from how you interpret experiences to how you align with your God-given destiny.

This scientific truth mirrors John 15:2, where Jesus says that fruitful branches are pruned to bear more fruit, and unfruitful ones are removed. Spiritually, you are being refined just like your brain keeping what is fruitful and cutting what is not. Synaptogenesis shows us that repetition builds direction, and that's as true in the spirit as it is in the brain. So, rebuilding strong and long-lasting neural pathways depends on the repeated use.

The neural pathways that are rarely activated begin to weaken and eventually fade away, while those reinforced through repetition become stronger, forming faster, clearer pathways. This isn't just neurological it mirrors a deeply spiritual principle. In John 15:2, Jesus said, *"Every branch in me that does not bear fruit He takes away; and every branch that bears fruit He prunes, that it may bear more fruit."* Spiritually and mentally, growth comes not only by adding new truth, but by removing old patterns pruning thoughts, habits, and beliefs that no longer serve God's plan for your life. Just as the brain trims away what isn't helpful, the Holy Spirit trims away what isn't holy or fruitful. When you stop rehearsing old lies and no longer feed dysfunctional thinking, your brain begins to let go of those old neural ruts. In their place, new spiritual highways can be formed highways of righteousness, peace, faith, and clarity that allow you to move swiftly and purposefully toward your God-ordained future. When a neural pathway isn't used, it gradually dissolves, making space for more useful, updated connections.

Spiritually, this mirrors repentance and renewal. When you stop rehearsing the lies of the enemy and refuse to feed old habits, the brain begins to disconnect them. Simultaneously, you can intentionally begin to build up a new way of being based on God's truth. Ephesians 4:22–23 describe this spiritual renewal best by stating to accomplish God's spiritual renewal, we must *"Put off the old man... and be renewed in the spirit of your mind."*

Vignette 3: Old Memories-Blocking New Love

Sister Can't-Let-Go! had been divorced for 10 years but still replayed the moment her ex-husband left every time she tried to date again. Her brain had created a "fear loop" that equated love with betrayal. With a Christian counselor, she began tracing the memory, uprooting the lie, and **refusing to relive it**. In place of that mental loop, **Sister Can't-Let-Go!** began journaling. This is an attempt to capture the truth of her journey as she transforms from **Sister Can't-Let-Go!** To **Sister Ready-For-Love!** She writes, *"I am safe in love. I am not abandoned. I am pursued by heaven and prepared for healthy partnership."*

Over time, the flashbacks faded, and new hope took their place. She didn't just get over her pain she rewired her future. Now she is working on advancing revelations to her repetition to accelerate her spiritual growth.

Vignette 4: Repetition=Spiritual Acceleration

Brother Eagle-Eyes, a recovering addict, had tried for years to quit. But it wasn't until he received a prophetic word that confirmed his calling as a counselor that something shifted. With renewed vision like an eagle, he began pairing daily declarations (*"I am no longer bound"*) with repetition (*attending support groups, praying in the Spirit, memorizing Scripture*). He then added **Isaiah 40:31 as declaration of Renewed Strength and Elevation:** *"But those who wait on the Lord shall renew their strength; They shall mount up with wings like eagles, They shall run and not be weary, They shall walk and not faint."* **Brother Eagle-**Eyes saw this scripture as describing himself like eagles, those who rely on the Lord gain supernatural endurance and elevation, rising above life's storms rather than being overcome by them. The combination of **discipline + revelation** caused a spiritual momentum that rewired his brain and rebuilt his life.

You are not stuck. Your patterns can be changed. Your thoughts can be transformed. And your future can be rewired to match your purpose. God has already written your destiny Now it's time to train your brain to carry it out your spiritual renewal with visual scripting and spiritual imagination.

4.2.   Spiritual Acceleration

Neural science tells us that it takes 21–60 days of repeated action to form or break a habit. But when repetition is partnered with revelation from the Holy Spirit, change happens not just faster but deeper. Revelation causes the heart to believe what the mind is practicing. That's when new thoughts stop being "hopeful statements" and start becoming spiritual legislation.

There is growing evidence in the fields of neurotheology, spiritual psychology, and faith-based behavioral therapy that spiritual practices (especially those involving the Holy Spirit) accelerate emotional healing, habit transformation and mental renewal.

It is widely accepted in behavioral science that forming or breaking a habit typically takes **an**

average of 21 to 60 days, depending on consistency, emotional intensity, and context (Lally et al., 2009). This process is rooted in **neuroplasticity** repetition and reward system in the brain's ability to form new neural pathways and weaken old ones. However, when repetition is partnered with revelation particularly through Holy Spirit-led prayer, prophetic insight, or divine conviction believers often experience faster internal alignment with truth and supernatural assistance in resisting old patterns.

Scripture confirms this principle when John 6:63 says, *"It is the Spirit who gives life; the flesh profits nothing. The words that I speak to you are spirit, and they are life."* And 2 Corinthians 3:18 *"But we all... are being transformed into the same image from glory to glory, just as by the Spirit of the Lord."* These verses suggest that the transformative work of the Holy Spirit doesn't bypass the brain but enhances its renewal process by infusing spiritual truth with supernatural grace.

Many Christians report that when a new habit is rooted not just in willpower, but in Spirit-empowered revelation, change comes faster, more deeply, and with longer-lasting impact. For example, a person struggling with pornography addiction may go through months of behavior modification with minimal results. But after receiving a Holy Spirit revelation about their identity, purity, and calling, the habit is not only broken faster it's replaced by new disciplines like worship, journaling, and Scripture meditation. The key difference is that the Holy Spirit rewrites the root, not just the behavior.

While there is no peer-reviewed study specifically saying, *"Holy Spirit causes faster habit formation,"* some research points toward spiritual engagement as a powerful accelerator of behavior change. Neurotheology (Dr. Andrew Newberg) studies on '*How God Changes Your Brain*' use brain imaging to show that prayer and spiritual meditation activate unique areas of the brain associated with emotional regulation, focus, and compassion suggesting that spiritual engagement enhances neuroplasticity and the brain's ability to change. His study also showed that religious and spiritual practices seem to strengthen the brain circuits involved in emotion regulation, attention, and processing of beliefs. In addition, **Faith-Based Recovery Programs (e.g., Celebrate Recovery, Teen Challenge)** report higher success rates in habit transformation and relapse prevention than secular counterparts. The key factor is that encounter with God, emotional healing through the Holy Spirit, and identity transformation through Scripture. Other words, your brain forms spiritual pathways when your spirit establishes repetitive behaviors to pave the road to your destiny.

There may not yet be a study that quantifies how fast the Holy Spirit rewires the brain, but countless testimonies and the Word itself reveal this truth, what takes the natural brain weeks to shift, the Spirit can accelerate in a moment of revelation. Because grace doesn't just heal it rewires for spiritual renewal.

4.3. Spiritual Renewal

Your spirit sees further than your situation if you allow it to dream with God. Vision scripting and spiritual imagination is just that, see it through God's eyes and you can have it.

Spiritual renewal isn't just about healing from what it was; it's about building toward what's next. And one of the most overlooked tools for doing that is the God-given gift of vision scripting partnering with the Holy Spirit to write down the future you are called to live. When coupled with **sanctified imagination**, vision scripting becomes more than goal setting it becomes **prophetic construction**. It is how you pull the unseen realm of heaven's intentions into the framework of your current life. Science describes it this way, your brain believes what you visualize.

Therefore, Neuroscience confirms that the brain doesn't distinguish much between what you *experience* and what you *vividly imagine.* When you mentally rehearse a future scenario, your brain begins firing as if it's real laying down neural blueprints for action and emotion. That means when you consistently script and imagine a healed, aligned, purposeful life, your brain begins to build the internal architecture to support it. The scientific also supports the biblical foundation of God uses vision to renew the spirit.

Habakkuk 2:2 proclaim, *"Write the vision, and make it plain on tablets, that he may run who reads it."* And Ephesians 3:20 declares, *"Now to Him who is able to do exceedingly abundantly above all that we ask or think, according to the power that works in us."* Thus, the Word of God invites us to think, imagine, and co-create with heaven not through fantasy, but through Spirit-breathed expectation. Vision scripting is not about daydreaming, it's about documenting destiny. Vision scripting is spiritual practice. This is why God often showed people visions before giving them instructions. Vision prepares the heart for obedience. It preps the pathway your soul will later walk.

Vision scripting is the intentional act of inviting the Holy Spirit into your imagination. Asking the Holy Spirit to show you what your life looks like healed, whole, and aligned. And writing down that vision in specific, personal, faith-filled language. Your script may include how you wake up, how you speak, how you lead, love, parent, give, serve, create, and live. Every time you review or rehearse that script; you are building spiritual highways and mental blueprints that align your future with heaven's reality. Heaven's reality is exercised in spiritual imagination that redeems our dreams.

Your imagination is not just a creative tool, it's a spiritual portal. Many people surrender their imagination to fear, anxiety, or fantasy. But when surrendered to God, imagination becomes the canvas where heaven paints pictures of what's possible. 1 Corinthians 2:9 *"Eye has not seen, nor ear heard... the things which God has prepared for those who love Him."* This spiritual truth gives us a glimpse into spiritual imagination that allows you to visualize freedom before it's felt, envision purpose before it's manifested and embrace identity before it's affirmed externally. We see Brother Eagle-Eyes in Vignette 4, go from scarcity to overflow. **Brother Eagle-Eyes**, after decades of addiction and survival thinking, began practicing vision scripting with the guidance of a spiritual mentor. And you can too.

Every morning, **Brother Eagle-Eyes** read aloud a vision script titled *"My Redeemed Life."* It described him mentoring young men, building a retreat center, and walking in supernatural purity. Over time, he began to **see** that the future in his spirit and his habits, words, and expectations followed. Today, he's living that script. Why? Because he wrote it in alignment with heaven and his soul caught up. Just imagine what your life would look like if you partnered with the Spirit to imagine, script, and declare it.

Let the Spirit show you what to plant.

Your pen is prophetic.

Your imagination is sacred.

Your future is not a gamble, it's a garden.

Before God ever formed the world, He imagined it. He spoke it. And then He saw it.

Your imagination isn't fantasy, it's a faculty.

Your imagination is your God-given tool for creating what hasn't yet appeared. Take time to write out your vision. Describe your future self. What do you see, hear, smell, feel? Vision scripting turns your imagination into instruction. You're not daydreaming, you're designing to build a lifestyle of positive repetition and habits.

Your life flows in the direction of your habits. The small decisions you make daily become the structure of your future. Start simple: wake up with intention, declare truth, journal your gratitude, eat with energy in mind, schedule time for your dreams. The more you repeat a behavior that aligns with your purpose, the deeper the groove becomes.

Repetition Rewires.

Discipline Delivers.

4.3.1. The Domino Effect of Deletion

Remember the spiritual weight of erasing and deleting? When you erase what was written whether in thought, word, or habit three things happen. Firstly, the word is removed from the script of your life, the thought begins to lose its power, and the root that once produced it is disrupted. Your future cannot manifest what no longer exists in your spirit. This is why consistent deletion and intentional reprogramming are vital. You're not just changing behaviors you're updating your spiritual software. Updating your spiritual software to rewire your future captures the domino effect of deletion and its transformative power in the soul, mind, and spirit.

Every word you think, speak, or write carries a form of spiritual coding. It doesn't just sit on paper, it gets stored in your inner archive, influencing how you live, decide, love, react, and believe. That's why deletion spiritually and mentally is not a small act. It is a system override, triggering a domino effect that doesn't just erase language it untangles roots, breaks agreements, and begins updating your spiritual operating system. The supernatural sequence unfolds in a couple of ways. (1) Deleting Negative Words from Your Script, (2) Thoughts Begins to Lose Their Power (3) Disrupted Roots (4) Deleting Negative Words from Your Script

When you delete a word be it *"I can't," "I'll always be alone," "I'm not good enough,"* or *"I'll never change"* you are removing a line of code from the script that governs your internal narrative. That single phrase may have built an entire behavioral pattern, emotional response, or limiting mindset. But when it is called out, rejected, and deleted, you are declaring that it no longer has a right to write about your life. The bible declares it this way, *"Let the weak say, 'I am strong.'"* (Joel 3:10).

By choosing new language rooted in truth, you begin to author a new script one that aligns with heaven's vocabulary, not hell's accusations. That deletion is your declaration: *"This lie is no longer my narrator."* For example, someone who always says, *"I sabotage every opportunity,"* when they delete that statement and replaces it with *"I am learning to steward every opportunity with wisdom and grace"* they immediately begin writing a new inner policy that informs their outer world.

Rewire Your Thoughts

Words don't live alone, they are fueled by thoughts, which are fed by repetition and belief. Once a word is deleted, the neural pathway that kept activating it begins to weaken. The brain stops reinforcing that idea. And spiritually, you've just revoked the enemy's access to that part of your identity. Scripture strengthens this point by letting us know to *"Take every thought captive to obey Christ."* (2 Corinthians 10:5).

This is spiritual neuroplasticity, as you refuse to rehearse the thought, the pathway that once made that belief feel automatic is dismantled. You don't just stop saying it, you stop *thinking about it with power.* It might still whisper, but it won't command. This is where consistency matters every time you refuse to feed the thought, you weaken its authority. For example, if you consistently deleted the phrase, *"I'm invisible,"* your thoughts gradually stopped jumping to that default in meetings, friendships, or even prayer. Why? Because you will stop feeding the lie with her words and the thought begin to wither from disuse.

4.3.2. ROOT: Once Produced is Disrupted

Every toxic word and thought are anchored in

a deeper root, a belief or experience that gave birth to the pattern. When you delete the word and stop empowering the thought, you begin to starve the root system that once fed it. Spiritually, this is what breaks generational cycles, emotional dysfunction, and identity distortions. Matthew 15:13 gives us the mind of God on this matter. It says, *"Every plant which My heavenly Father has not planted will be uprooted."*

What you stop rehearsing, you stop watering. And when you refuse to write, speak, or think in alignment with that root, the entire system starts to collapse. Your identity becomes detached from the pain, and your soul becomes fertile ground for truth to grow. For example, if you once believed *"I'm just like my father angry, cold, unreachable,"* intentionally delete every thought and phrase connected to that identity. Over time, not only will your mindset shift, but your emotional triggers softened. You will not only become a better man you will became a new one. The root of inherited pain lost its grip because the spiritual system feeding it had been disrupted.

You are not just changing behaviors; you are updating your spiritual software. This is why deletion is more than emotional, it's technical, spiritual, and neurological. When you begin removing old programming one word, one belief, one memory at a time you are initiating a total system update. The Holy Spirit is not just tweaking your behavior; He is replacing your inner coding with truth, grace, and divine strategy.

You are no longer operating on fear-based software. You are no longer navigating life using a corrupt system. You are being renewed, rewritten and realigned, line, law by law, root by root to design your environment.

4.4. Designing Your Environment

Designing your environment to support transformation is as planting new seeds into fertile ground. You shouldn't plant new seeds in toxic soil. Your environment matters. This is the same as the scripture that tells us that we shouldn't place new wine into old wineskins.

When it comes to spiritual renewal and lasting transformation, your environment must match your evolution. Jesus illustrated this perfectly when He said, *"No one puts new wine into old wineskins. Otherwise, the new wine will burst the skins, it will spill, and the skins will be ruined"*(Luke

5:37). The imagery is clear. New substances cannot thrive in old structures.

Wineskins, made from animal hide, would stretch as the wine fermented. Once used, they became brittle and inflexible. Pouring fresh wine into an old, rigid skin would cause both to be lost. The same is true for your inner growth. You cannot expect a renewed mind or healed identity to flourish in an unchanged, toxic, or limiting environment. Whether it's the relationships you keep, the routines you follow, the spaces you live in, or the emotional climates you tolerate your surroundings must be restructured to hold what God is pouring into you. Designing your environment for transformation means identifying what can no longer contain the new version of you. That includes mindsets, media, conversations, habits, and atmospheres. New seeds require new soil. New vision needs fresh infrastructure. You cannot carry prophetic vision while living in patterns of your past. What you're building in you must be supported by around you.

What are you listening to? Who are you surrounded by? What visuals dominate your space? Curate your surroundings to reflect where you're going, not where you've been. Change the music, clean your space, surround yourself with life-givers and truth-speakers. You grow where you're nurtured, not where you're merely planted. In this case, faith plus works helps you to walk into the future you've declared.

Faith without work is dead, and declarations without decisions are empty. If you've spoken about your new future, walk it out. Apply for the program; Send the email; Start the business; Go to therapy; Launch the podcast. Faith is forward motion powered by trust. Partner your declarations with dedication. Activation of your faith is your future self-blueprint + prophetic decrees.

Say it.

Believe it.

Walk it.

Take time to complete your Future Self Blueprint by answering:

- Who is the future version of me?
- What does my daily routine look like in the future?
- What decisions does my future self-make consistently?

- What must I let go of today to step into that version?
- What must I say yes to today to become them?

Now speak these Prophetic Decrees Over Your Destiny out loud:

- I am not who I was.
- I am becoming who.
- I'm called to be.
- My future is fertile ground, and I sow in faith.
- I write my reality with Heaven's ink.
- I erase what no longer serves and decree what aligns with God's Word.
- My destiny is secure, my steps are ordered, and my future is bright.

You're no longer a victim of patterns you're a programmer of purpose. You've deleted what's broken, rooted out what's hidden, rewritten what's present, and now you're walking in a future authored by God and co-signed by your obedience. Now you need the perfect seal. The seal of the Reset is returning to the original design.

4.4.1. THE RESET

The Reset is the sacred pause where transformation begins. It is more than a moment of reflection it's a spiritual and mental intervention that allows you to disconnect from the cycle of your past and recalibrate your internal systems to match heaven's intention for your future. Just like a frozen or malfunctioning computer needs a reboot to clear corrupted processes, restore functionality, and reestablish connection to its original operating system, your soul often needs a RESET to break free from old emotional programs, soul traffic, or toxic behavioral loops. Spiritually, a reset is an act of humility and alignment. It's saying, "God, I'm ready to let go of what isn't working and surrender to what You originally designed for me." Resetting doesn't erase who you are—it clears the clutter that's been corrupting who you're meant to become.

To experience a true reset, you must first identify the glitches in your thought patterns, those recurring lies, limiting beliefs, and self-sabotaging behaviors that keep rerouting your destiny. Then, you unplug from your default reactions by choosing stillness, repentance, rest, or intentional silence. Whether through fasting, solitude, or Spirit-led prayer, the reset moment breaks the power of autopilot. This gives space for the Holy Spirit to reconnect you to your original programming your identity as a son or daughter of God, rooted in truth, free from fear, and filled with purpose.

Resetting is not passive. It requires that you take authority over what's been running in the background of your life. You must evict old narratives, clean up corrupted thought files, and reinstall the language, habits, and agreements that align with God's vision. Only then can you begin the process of rewiring your future with clarity and power. The reset doesn't mean going back to who you were, it means returning to who you were always meant to be.

4.4.2. RESET PRAYER CARDS

Awesome! Here's a set of seven (7) reset prayer cards of DELETE TH@T. Each card includes a targeted prayer that aligns with the theme of the chapter, written in a voice that matches the book: personal, prophetic, and spiritually grounded.

PRAYER CARD 1: Deleting Negative Patterns
Scripture: Proverbs 18:21, Romans 12:2
Prayer: DELETE TH@T - Negative Mind, Mouth & Movement

Father, in the name of Jesus, I surrender every toxic thought, careless word, and sabotaging action that does not align with Your truth. Expose the loops I've been trapped in. Reveal the words I *speak that bind me to bondage. Break every agreement I've made with fear, lack, and shame knowingly or unknowingly. I receive the power of Your Word to renew my mind, cleanse my mouth, and guide my movement. Today, I boldly say: DELETE TH@T. I am ready to think, speak, and walk in truth. Amen.*

PRAYER CARD 2: ROOT IT OUT

Theme: Uprooting the Past

Scripture: Proverbs 25:28, Jeremiah 1:10

Prayer:

Holy Spirit, search for the roots of my life. Reveal the generational patterns, childhood wounds, and silent agreements that keep me stuck. I choose to no longer bury pain. I invite You to excavate it. Cut off every root that produces fear, self-hate, pride, and limitation. I renounce what no longer serves me and embrace the healing You freely offer. My past will not govern my present. Uproot me, restore me, and replant me in righteousness. In Jesus' name, Amen.

PRAYER CARD 3: WRITE IT RIGHT

Theme: Rewriting the Present

Scripture: Hebrews 11:1, Proverbs 18:20-21

Prayer:

Lord, help me to write with wisdom. Let my words, thoughts, and self-talk reflect Heaven's opinion of me. Today, I erase every false identity I've accepted, and I rewrite my narrative with Your truth. I declare I am loved, I am worthy, I am chosen, and I am capable. Let my actions reflect my healed self. Help me walk in the rhythm of grace, not guilt. I choose to speak life over my now and step boldly into alignment. Amen.

PRAYER CARD 4: PROGRAM THE FUTURE

Theme: Rewiring the Future

Scripture: Romans 12:2, Isaiah 43:19

Prayer:

God, thank You that my future is not limited by my past. Today, I partner with You to rewire my future by faith. I write new vision, new declarations, and new decisions. Let my mind be renewed, my habits be holy, and my atmosphere be fertile for purpose. Delete every lingering file of fear or doubt. I declare the future is open, the path is clear, and the code I live by is truth. I will walk in the destiny You authored for me boldly, faithfully, and fearlessly. In

Jesus' name, Amen.

Would you like these formatted into printable or digital card designs (PDF or PNG)? I can create those next!

PRAYER CARD 5: RESET THE STANDARD

Theme: Breaking Agreements with Mediocrity

Scripture: Ephesians 3:20, 1 Peter 2:9

Prayer:

Father, I repent for agreeing with anything beneath what You've ordained for me. I break every subconscious vow I've made with mediocrity, fear of success, and playing small. I am not average. I am anointed. I am not stuck. I am sent. I declare that I will no longer settle where You've called me to soar. Elevate my expectations. Expand my vision. Align my life with Your supernatural standard. In Jesus' name, Amen.

PRAYER CARD 6: SILENCE THE SABOTEUR

Theme: Taking Authority Over Inner Criticism

Scripture: 2 Corinthians 10:5, Philippians 4:8

Prayer:

Lord, today I take authority over every voice internal or external that speaks against who You created me to be. I silence the critic, the cynic, the imposter within. I cast down arguments and every high thing that exalts itself against the knowledge of You in me. I choose thoughts of faith, purity, power, and peace. Let my mind become a sanctuary of truth and confidence. I will no longer sabotage my future with yesterday's fear. In Jesus' name, Amen.

PRAYER CARD 7: CLEAN THE ALTAR

Theme: Removing Contamination from Sacred Spaces

Scripture: Psalm 51:10, Romans 12:1

Prayer:

Holy Spirit, search every area of my heart that I've polluted with pride, bitterness, or compromise. Clean the altar of my life. Let my motives be pure, my intentions be right, and my worship be authentic. I present my body, mind, and spirit as a living sacrifice. Burn away what dishonors You and restore what pleases You. I will consecrate myself again today. I am Yours, wholly and fully.

[Here is the link to ACTIVITY 16: Images of Prayer Cards.](#)

With these cards, your Future Is Programmable. You will be able to have these truths at your digital fingerprints as a reference to writing the Right Code, capturing the heart of the chapter while reinforcing the key transformational insights.

Throughout this chapter, you've learned the powerful truth that your future isn't fixed it's programmable, and you are the architect.

Through the science of neuroplasticity and the renewing work of the Holy Spirit, you've learned that lasting transformation begins in the mind and is reinforced through consistent thought, words, and action. You now understand how to interrupt old patterns, overwrite limiting beliefs, and design new mental and spiritual highways that carry your destiny.

We explored tools like vision scripting, spiritual imagination, habitual repetition, and the sacred power of a spiritual reset each designed to help you break free from autopilot living and intentionally code your future with faith, strategy, and divine alignment. The words you choose, the thoughts you entertain, and the movements you repeat all build the path you walk. Now equipped with the revelation that you're not just living, you're leading your future, you're ready to step into what's next with clarity, boldness, and renewed authority to rewire your future.

CONCLUSION: Delete It for Good

You've walked through every layer mind, mouth, and movement confronting and deleting toxic patterns that once dictated your pace, identity, and perspective. You've learned that what you write, think, speak, and repeat are not meaningless moments; they are blueprints for your life. Your self-talk was never just private commentary, it was prophecy in motion. But now, you've been given the tools to rewrite the script. To uproot old narratives, uninstall limiting beliefs, reprogram your internal language, and build a future that reflects who God says you are not who pain tried to make you. The journey of deleting is not about erasing your past, it's about reclaiming your authority over what stays, what goes, and what governs your soul moving forward.

Now, responsibility and privileges are yours. You are the keeper of your soul's government, the author of your spiritual policies, and the architect of your internal environment. You're no longer living under old decrees; you're writing new declarations that echo in heaven and manifest on earth. Let every thought be vetted, every word be intentional, and every step be prophetic. And when old patterns try to resurface, don't argue with them **DELETE TH@T**. You are no longer a passive participant in your own life. You are an active co-creator with God. And as you continue this work of renewal, remember you are not just breaking cycles, you're birthing legacy. Keep writing the truth. Keep uprooting lies. And keep programming a future that aligns with the freedom, favor, and fulfillment that God has already prepared for you

ACTIVITIES & EXERCISES

ACTIVITY 1: Tracing Pre-Memory Patterns

1. **Reflect on Your Birth Story**
   - Ask your parents or guardians what the pregnancy and birth experience was like.
   - Were there complications, stress, or fears surrounding your birth?
   - How did your parents feel when they found out they were expecting you?

2. **Journal Prompts**
   - Do I struggle with rejection, fear, or feeling like a burden?
   - Are there emotions I carry that seem older than my memories?
   - Have I always felt pressure to perform or prove myself?

3. **Holy Spirit Activation**
   - Invite the Holy Spirit to reveal the origin of certain emotions or patterns.
   - Write down anything that comes to mind without judgment. These impressions may be the Holy Spirit surfacing buried roots.

4. **Declaration**
    - Speak this aloud: *"I am not bound to what happened before I was born. I am anchored in what God says about me now. My beginnings are blessed, my design is divine, and my identity is secure in Christ."*

EXERCISE 2: Passing Good Epigenetics

How to Intentionally Pass on Good Epigenetics

1. **Live What You Want to Be Inherited:** *Your children are not just watching; they're absorbing your patterns. When you live by the Spirit, they inherit a blueprint of alignment.*

2. **Pray Into Your Bloodline:** *Speak blessings over your descendants now even those not yet born. Your words become **spiritual seeds.***

3. **Break Negative Cycles + Plant New Ones:** *When you break a curse, replace it with a blessing. When you DELETE TH@T, replace it with truth, identity, and legacy.*

4. **Create Atmospheres of Peace and Presence:** *Worship in your home. Speak life. Practice joy. Those moments matter **more than any curriculum or counseling session.***

EXERCISE 3: Healing Inherited Patterns

1. Recognize the Pattern

Ask God to reveal invisible agreements or emotions that feel "too big" or "too old" to belong to your personal story.

- Prayer: *"Holy Spirit, is there a generational pattern or inherited emotion that I've accepted as mine?"*
- Journaling Prompt: *What emotions or behaviors do I experience that don't match my known experiences?*

2. Renounce the Agreement

You must break agreement with inherited lies, fear, and trauma in the spirit realm.

- Prayer:
"In Jesus' name, I renounce every emotional pattern, lie, or fear that was passed down to me through my bloodline. I cancel every assignment of inherited trauma. I am not in covenant with pain. I am in covenant with healing."

3. Replace the Programming with God's Truth

Declare what God says about your identity, legacy, and freedom.

- Declaration:

  "I am not who my family's pain says I am. I am not the trauma of those before me. I am a new creation. I am stable, secure, and loved. I have a sound mind and a redeemed legacy." Scripture: 2 Corinthians 5:17: *"If anyone is in Christ, he is a new creation..."* & Galatians 3:13: *"Christ redeemed us from the curse..."*

4. Engage in Therapeutic Healing: Spiritual healing is powerful, but **renewal is also neurological**. Work with a trauma-informed therapist or counselor. Combine therapeutic sessions with inner healing prayer and Scripture meditation

ACTIVITY 4: DELETE TH@T – Language

DELETE TH@T" Language Checklist

Use this checklist to **catch and replace** common self-sabotaging speech. I encourage you to add your own phrases to this checklist and intentionally **"DELETE TH@T"** in real-time by replacing it with truth.

❌ DELETE TH@T Phrase	✅ Speak This Instead
"I'm always messing	"I'm learning, growing, and

❌ DELETE TH@T Phrase	✅ Speak This Instead
up."	improving daily."
"I don't have what it takes."	"God equips me for every good work."
"Nothing ever works out for me."	"All things are working together for my good."
"I'm just like my dysfunctional parent."	"I break generational cycles and walk in freedom."
"That's just the way I am."	"I am being transformed by the renewing of my mind."
"Nobody wants me."	"I am seen, chosen, and deeply loved by God."
"I'm broke."	"Provision follows purpose. God supplies my need."
"I can't do this."	"I can do all things through Christ who strengthens me."

EXERCISE 5: 7-DAY Anti-Self-Sabotage

7 Days of Vocal Confession to Deliver My Mouth

For any 7-day cycle, commit to monitoring your words and rewriting your declarations. Each morning, confess the truth out loud. Each night, reflect on any words you need to *DELETE TH@T* and reframe them.

Try to go **7 days without saying anything self-sabotaging**. If you do, restart the challenge!

Instructions:

1. **Set a reminder** each morning: *"My mouth sets my atmosphere today."*
2. **Use a small journal or phone notes** to track:
   - What you almost said
   - What you caught yourself saying
   - How you corrected it
3. **At the end of each day**, write down 1 phrase you deleted and 1 new declaration you replaced it with.
4. **Every night**, speak this aloud:

"Today, I chose life. I chose truth. My voice is a tool for freedom, not failure."

Daily Steps:

1. Begin your day with a scripture-based declaration (see below).

2. Avoid phrases like "I'm broke," "I'm tired of life," "I'll never," "It's always like this."
3. When a negative phrase slips, pause, say "DELETE TH@T," and restate the truth.
4. Journal what words you caught and what truth you replaced them with.

Suggested Scriptures to Declare:

- *"I am the head and not the tail."* – Deut. 28:13
- *"I am fearfully and wonderfully made."* – Ps. 139:14
- *"Let the weak say, 'I am strong.'"* – Joel 3:10
- *"I can do all things through Christ."* – Phil. 4:13

ACTIVITY 6: Behavioral Cycles & Movement

Instructions: Behavioral Cycles / Movement Worksheet

Take a moment of quiet reflection. With honesty and no self-condemnation, list your repeated behaviors and what they reveal about your inner agreements.

Repeated Behavior	When/Why It Happens	What I Often Say or Think Before It	What I Know God Says Instead
Example: Avoiding hard conversations	When I fear rejection	"They won't understand me"	"God gives me boldness and clarity"

After adding the behaviors, you want to surrender, ask God to begin renewing the thoughts and beliefs behind them.

EXERCISE 7: Behavior vs. Belief Alignment

This exercise will help you confront incongruent actions and bring alignment to your walk, words, and beliefs.

Instructions: Behavior vs Belief Alignment

Match your outward behavior with the belief that fuels it. Then challenge it with God's truth.

Behavior I Keep Repeating	Belief That Supports It	Is This Belief True?	New Truth I Choose to Believe
Procrastinating on purpose	"I'll probably fail anyway"	✗	"God has equipped me for success."
Staying in toxic relationships	"This is the best I can get"	✗	"I am worth healthy, God-ordained love."

This exercise is designed to reveals what you may be unconsciously agreeing with and gives you a simple format to rewrite the narrative in real time.

ACTIVITY 8: Who's Ruling in My Soul?

- What kind of thoughts have been legislating my

internal world lately? Are they rooted in truth or fear?

- What do my words say about who holds authority in my life?
- What patterns or habits am I living out that reflect an old law or agreement?
- What have I written, posted, or declared that might need to be "deleted" or rewritten?
- What new decree do I need to write today to begin living in alignment with God's truth?

Use these questions to assess the governance of your soul.

ACTIVITY 9: 3-Gate Reflection

3-Gate Reflection activity (Think–Speak–Write)

Gate 1: THINK – The Thought Filter

"Be transformed by the renewing of your mind..." – Romans 12:2

- What recurring thoughts have I allowed that are rooted in fear, shame, or insecurity?
- Where did those thoughts originate—childhood? trauma? culture? comparison?

- Have I accepted any of these thoughts as permanent truths rather than patterns to be broken?
- What is one toxic thought I need to confront and submit to God's truth today?

DECLARATION: *"I cast down every imagination and thought that rises against the knowledge of God. I think on what is true, noble, right, pure, lovely, admirable, excellent, and praiseworthy. My thoughts are holy ground."*

Gate 2: SPEAK – The Speech Audit

"Death and life are in the power of the tongue..." – Proverbs 18:21

- What have I been saying about myself, my future, or others that I wouldn't want to come true?
- Do my words reflect God's promises or my pain?
- When I feel stressed, disappointed, or unsure— what is my default language?
- What declarations have I spoken that need to be "deleted" and replaced with truth?

DECLARATION: *"I silence the voice of fear, lack, and limitation. My mouth speaks life, blessing, healing, and alignment with God's Word. I am a prophetic vessel, and my words build the future God has promised me."*

Gate 3: WRITE – The Scribe's Authority

"Write the vision and make it plain..." – Habakkuk 2:2

- What have I written in journals, texts, captions, or notes that reinforce a wounded identity?
- Have I written out hopelessness in ink that should've been surrendered in prayer?
- What declarations, affirmations, or Scriptures can I write daily to establish a new foundation?
- If my journal were a blueprint, would it reflect heaven's design or my past disappointments?

DECLARATION: *"I break agreement with every written word that does not align with truth. I reclaimed my scribe's authority. My pen is prophetic. I write the vision, the healing, and the destiny God has spoken over my life."*

ACTIVITY 10: Spiritual Excavation

1. IDENTIFY THE NEGATIVE BELIEF

What thought or internal message keeps resurfacing that you know isn't serving your growth?

Example: "I'm not good enough," "I'll always be broke," "People always leave me."

My Belief: _____

2. NAME THE EMOTION

What feeling is most often attached to this belief?

Examples: fear, shame, anger, sadness, insecurity.

Emotion(s): _____

3. TRACE THE ORIGIN

When did you first start feeling or believing this?

Was there a moment, conversation, or experience that planted this seed?

The First Memory I Can Recall:_____

_____

4. WHO OR WHAT PLANTED THE SEED?

Was it something a parent, teacher, friend, or culture made you believe?

Was it connected to trauma, abandonment, rejection, or failure?

Root Source:_____

5. WHAT HAS THIS ROOT PRODUCED IN YOUR LIFE?

How has this belief affected your relationships, decisions, habits, or sense of self-worth?

Impact/Fruit:_____

6. WHAT IS THE TRUTH?

Replace the lie with a truth that aligns with God's Word and your divine identity.

Example: "I am chosen and equipped," "I have more than enough," "I am safe and loved."

New Belief/Declaration:_____

7. PRAY & RENOUNCE

Speak this prayer aloud and mean it from your heart:

"Holy Spirit, I give You full access to the hidden places of my heart. I renounce this belief and every root it grew from. I no longer agree with lies that limit who I am or who I'm becoming. Uproot what has been planted by pain, and replace it with truth, healing, and your divine perspective. I am not my past. I am not my trauma. I am not the lie, I am Your masterpiece. In Jesus' name, Amen."

ACTIVITY 11: Trace The Root

Root Tracing Worksheet: What's Beneath This?

Step 1: Identify the Fruit (Visible Reaction or Pattern)

- What did I say, feel, or do that seem out of alignment with who I want to be?

Example: I shut down in conversations when I feel challenged.

Step 2: Explore the Trigger (What Happened Just Before?)

- What was said, done, or remembered that led to that response?

Example: Someone gave me honest feedback and I felt exposed.

Step 3: Locate the Belief

- What belief or thought surfaced in that moment?

Example: "I'm not safe when I'm vulnerable."

Step 4: Trace the Root

- Where did this belief come from? Is there a memory, relationship, or repeated experience tied to it?

Example: Childhood moments where I was mocked for expressing myself.

Step 5: Invite the Holy Spirit to Speak Truth

- Ask: "Holy Spirit, what do You say about this?" Write the truth He reveals.

Example: "Your voice is valuable. I've given you wisdom, and you are safe with Me."

Step 6: Replace the Old Script

- What new declaration or truth can you speak over this area going forward?

Example: "I am safe to be seen, and my vulnerability is a strength, not a liability."

ACTIVITY 12: Legislation Thought Tracker

ACTIVITY: Personal Legislation-Thought Tracker

Write down 3 thoughts you've been repeating internally. For each, ask:

1. Is this thought biblical or emotional?
2. Does this thought reflect fear or faith?
3. Where did I first begin to believe this?
4. What would I rather believe in agreement with God?

Example Thought: "I'm not good enough."

- ❌ Origin: Childhood rejection
- ✅ Replacement: "I am accepted in the Beloved and complete in Christ" (Ephesians 1:6, Colossians 2:10)

ACTIVITY 13: Self-Healing Language

Intentional Self-Healing Language

- **Write Your Old Story**: List out the limiting beliefs, repeated phrases, or labels you've lived under.
- **Cross Them Out One by One**: Physically draw a line through each one.
- **Write Your New Story**: For each lie, write a truth that reflects who you really are.
- Then begin this simple Daily Renewal Ritual:
- Speak your top 3 declarations aloud.
- Take 3 deep breaths to reset.
- **Ask yourself**: "What is one aligned action I can take today?"
- Commit to doing it before the day ends.

ACTIVITY 14: DISCERNMENT DETECTOR

DISCERNMENT DETECTOR: "Lie, Law, or the Lord?"

This discernment detector acts as a spiritual filter to help us evaluate the origin and authority behind our thoughts. Here is how it works:

(1) Lie: Ask: *"Is this thought a deception?"* Is it rooted in fear, shame, trauma, insecurity, or past experiences? Or if it contradicts Scripture or produces anxiety, isolation, or hopelessness it's a lie. These thoughts often sound like:

- *"I'll never be enough."*
- *"God is disappointed in me."*

- *"I don't deserve healing."*

(2) Law: Ask: *"Is this thought a self-imposed rule I created to protect myself?"* This is a belief that may have served as emotional survival in a hard season but is now governing your behavior in unhealthy ways. It's not necessarily evil, but it's not freedom. It's a self-made law that needs to be reviewed, revised, or repealed. These thoughts sound like:

- *"I can't trust anyone."*
- *"I must do everything myself."*
- *"I have to earn love."*

(3) Lord: Ask: *"Is this thought submitted to the authority and truth of God?"* These thoughts reflect the mind of Christ and align with Scripture. This is truth governed by the Lord. This is the voice you want ruling your mind. They bring peace, conviction (not condemnation), clarity, and direction. These sound like:

- *"God is with me, even here."*
- *"I am forgiven and being transformed."*
- *"His plans for me are good."*

So, when a thought enters, simply ask: Is this a LIE I've believed, a LAW I've enforced, or a truth from the LORD? This simple filter empowers readers to reclaim thought authority and align their soul with truth.

ACTIVITY 15: Future Self Script

Step 1: Write in Present Tense: Speak as though you are already living in the reality God is calling you into.

Instead of: "I hope I become confident." **Write:** "I am bold, secure, and unshakable in my identity."

Step 2: Use This Framework

My Mind (Thoughts I Believed):

I think in alignment with God's truth. I no longer default to fear or insecurity. I welcome clarity, peace, and vision into every decision.

Write Your Version: *"My mind is..."*

_____

My Mouth (Words About Myself & Others):

I speak about life, not limitations.

I no longer repeat the lies of the past.

My words create solutions, not cycles.

Write Your Version: *"My mouth is..."*

_____

My Movement (How I Live, Act, and Choose):

I walk in purpose and courage.

DELETE TH@T

I make decisions that align with my future, not my fear.

I honor my time, my body, and my relationships.

Write Your Version: *"My daily life reflects..."*

My Identity (Who I Know I Am):

I am whole, chosen, wise, and loved. I am no longer who trauma tried to make me. I am the healed version of me. I lead from overflow, not emptiness.

Write Your Version: *"I am..."*

My Future (Where I'm Headed and Who I'm Becoming):

I am stepping into rooms God has prepared for me. My future is fruitful, focused, and filled with peace. I have divine rhythm, unstoppable favor, and lasting impact.

Write Your Version: *"I see my future becoming..."*

ACTIVITY 16: VISUAL PRAYER CARDS 1-7

DELETE TH@T

ACTIVITIES & EXERCISES

PRAYER CARD 1
Scripture Anchor: Proverbs 18:21

Lord, make me aware of the negativity I speak. I repent for speaking words that do not reflect love, gratitude, or faith. I delete complaining, criticism, and judgment from my lips. Let my mouth bring life and not death, blessing and not cursing. In Jesus' name, Amen.

PRAYER CARD 2
ROOT OUT THE PAST
Scripture Anchor 25:28, Jeremiah 1.10

Holy Spirit, search the roots of my life. Reveal the generational patterns, childhood wounds, and silent agreements that keep me stuck. Cut off every root that produces fear, self-hate, pride, and limitation. My past will not govern my present. In Jesus' name, Amen.

PRAYER CARD 3
WRITE IT RIGHT

SCRICTURE ANCHOR: Hebrews 11:1, Proverbs 18:20-21

Prayer: Lord, I rewrite the present with wisdom and my self-talk reflects Heaven's identity of me. I declare I am loved. I am worthy, I am chosen, and I am capable. I will walk in the rhythm of grace, not guilt. I choose to speak life over my now. Amen.

PRAYER CARD 4: REWRITE THE FUTURE

Scripture Anchor: Romans 12:2, Isaiah 43:19

God, thank You that my future is not limited by my past and you hewired my future. I DECLARE, My mind is renewed, my habits are holy, my atmosphere is fertile, and my path is clear. I will walk in the destiny You authored for me boldly, faithfully, and fearlessly. In Jesus' name, Amen.

PRAYER CARD 5:
RESET THE STANDARD

Scripture Anchor: Ephesians 3:20, 1Peter 2.9

Father, I repent for agreeing with anything beneath what You've ordained for me. I break every vow related to fear of success. I am not average, I am anointed. I declare that I will no longer settle where You've called me to soar. In Jesus' name, Amen.

PRAYER CARD 6
CONFESSION

Today, I DELETE every thought that does not align with Your truth, God. I CANCEL every self-sabotaging word I've spoken. I choose to walk in freedom, renewal, and divine alignment. In Jesus' name, Amen.

2 Corinthians 10:5 Taking Thoughts Captive

PRAYER CARD 7
CLEAN THE ALTAR

Scripture Anchor: Psalms 51:10, Romans 12.1

Prayer: Holy Spirit, search every area of my heart that I've polluted with pride, bitterness, or compromise. Clean the altar of my HEART so it emits pure, and authentic intentions. Burn away what dishonors You, and restore what pleases You. In Jesus' name, Amen.

Scripture Anchor: Ephesians 3:20, Philippians 4:8

SPEAK NO MORE

BONUS CARD
SILENCE THE SABOTEUR

Lord, today I take authority over every voice—internal or external—that speaks against who You created me to be. I silence the critic, the cynic, the imposter within. I cast down arguments and every high thing that exalts itself against the knowledge of You in me. I choose thoughts of faith, purity, power, and peace. Let my mind become a sanctuary of truth and confidence. I will no longer sabotage my future with yesterday's fear. In Jesus' name,

Bibliography

(1) American Psychological Association. *Stress in America™ 2020: A National Mental Health Crisis.* https://www.apa.org/news/press/releases/stress/2020/report

(2) Anolli, L., & Ciceri, R. (2017). Feeling Offended: A Blow to Our Image and Our Social Relationships. *Frontiers in Psychology*, 8, 570. https://doi.org/10.3389/fpsyg.2017.00570 PMC

(3) Bible. Authorized King James Version (KJV), Oxford UP, 1998.

(4) Bible. New International Version (NIV), Biblica, www.biblica.com/bible/, Accessed 3 April 2025.

(5) Bible. The Holy Bible: New Living Translation (NLT). Tyndale House Publishers, 2015.

(6) Carver, Charles S., and Michael F. Scheier. *On the Self-Regulation of Behavior.* Cambridge University Press, 1998.

(7) Cassidy, Jude, and Phillip R. Shaver, editors. *Handbook of Attachment: Theory, Research, and Clinical Applications.* 3rd ed., Guilford Press, 2016.

(8) Centers for Disease Control and Prevention. *Adverse Childhood Experiences (ACEs) Study.* 1998–2014. https://www.cdc.gov/violenceprevention/aces/index.html

(9) Eisenberger, Naomi I., Matthew D. Lieberman, and Kipling D. Williams. "Does Rejection Hurt? An fMRI Study of Social Exclusion." *Science*, vol. 302, no. 5643,

2003, pp. 290–292. https://doi.org/10.1126/science.1089134

(10) Fisher, Helen E., Arthur Aron, and Lucy L. Brown. "Romantic Love: A Mammalian Brain System for Mate Choice." Philosophical Transactions of the Royal Society B: Biological Sciences, vol. 361, no. 1476, 2006, pp. 2173–2186. https://doi.org/10.1098/rstb.2006.1938.

(11) Glover, Vivette. "Maternal Depression, Anxiety and Stress During Pregnancy and Child Outcome: What Needs to Be Done." *Best Practice & Research Clinical Obstetrics and Gynaecology*, vol. 25, no. 6, 2011, pp. 523–535. https://doi.org/10.1016/j.bpobgyn.2011.04.004

(12) Glover, Vivette. "Maternal Depression, Anxiety and Stress during Pregnancy and Child Outcome: What Needs to Be Done." *Best Practice & Research Clinical Obstetrics and Gynaecology*, vol. 28, no. 1, 2014, pp. 25–35. *Elsevier*, https://doi.org/10.1016/j.bpobgyn.2013.08.017.

(13) Huttenlocher, Peter R., and A. S. Dabholkar. "Regional Differences in Synaptogenesis in Human Cerebral Cortex." *The Journal of Comparative Neurology*, vol. 387, no. 2, 1997, pp. 167–178. Wiley Online Library, https://doi.org/10.1002/(SICI)1096-9861(19971020)387:2<167::AID-CNE1>3.0.CO;2-Z.

(14) Kays, Jillian L., Robert A. Hurley, and Katherine H. Taber. "The Dynamic Brain: Neuroplasticity and Mental Health." The Journal of Neuropsychiatry and Clinical Neurosciences, vol. 24, no. 2, 2012, pp. 118–124. https://doi.org/10.1176/appi.neuropsych.12070109

(15)   Lally, Phillippa, et al. "How Are Habits Formed: Modelling Habit Formation in the Real World." *European Journal of Social Psychology*, vol. 40, no. 6, 2009, pp. 998–1009. https://doi.org/10.1002/ejsp.674

(16)   Morris, Michael, and Clara Reiber. "Exploring Gender Differences in the Emotional Impact of Breakup." Evolutionary Psychology, vol. 9, no. 2, 2011, pp. 229–241. https://doi.org/10.1177/147470491100900206

(17)   Morris, Michael C., and Clara Reiber. "Exploring Gender Differences in the Emotional Impact of Breakup." Evolutionary Behavioral Sciences, vol. 11, no. 3, 2017, pp. 222–229. https://doi.org/10.1037/ebs0000103.

(18)   National Council for Mental Wellbeing. *Trauma and Recovery Resources.* 2020. https://www.thenationalcouncil.org

(19)   Newberg, Andrew B., and Mark Robert Waldman. *How God Changes Your Brain: Breakthrough Findings from a Leading Neuroscientist.* Ballantine Books, 2009.

(20)   Partanen, Eino, et al. "Learning-Induced Neural Plasticity of Speech Processing before Birth." *Proceedings of the National Academy of Sciences*, vol. 110, no. 37, 2013, pp. 15145–15150. *PNAS*, https://doi.org/10.1073/pnas.1302159110.

(21)   Oliffe, John L., et al. "Men's Mental Health Following Relationship Breakdowns: A Scoping Review." Journal of Men's Health, vol. 15, no. 1, 2019, pp. 17–25.

(22) Schwarz, J. (2020). Is There Such a Thing as an 'Offensive Picture'? *ResearchGate*.
https://www.researchgate.net/publication/344956974_Is_There_such_a_Thing_as_an_Offensive_Picture

(23)   Weaver, Ian C. G., et al. "Epigenetic Programming by Maternal Behavior." *Nature Neuroscience*, vol. 7, no. 8, 2004, pp. 847–854. https://doi.org/10.1038/nn1276.

Van der Kolk, Bessel A. *The Body Keeps the Score: Brain, Mind, and Body in the Healing of Trauma*. Penguin Books, 2014.

www.ingramcontent.com/pod-product-compliance
Lightning Source LLC
Chambersburg PA
CBHW061256110426
42742CB00012BA/1932